MORE
BLESSED
TO GIVE

MORE BLESSED TO GIVE

Straight Talk on Stewardship

JOHN H. MacNAUGHTON

 CHURCH

Church Publishing, New York

First published in 1975, under the title *Stewardship: Myth and Methods*
Reprinted in 1981, under the title *Money is Not a Four Letter Word*
Revised and updated, 1983

cover art: Robert Delaunay, *Windows, 1912*

Church Publishing Incorporated
445 Fifth Avenue
New York NY 10016

5 4 3 2 1

Contents

v

Prologue

It all began at the coffee hour following the morning service. Sam Bloom, the senior warden, cornered the rector, the Reverend Timothy O'Dell, at the coffee pot. After the usual morning pleasantries had been exchanged, Sam's tone changed from cheerfulness (it had been a good Sunday with familiar hymns, a good-sized congregation and an interesting sermon) to mild concern as he said, "Tim, I suppose we had better get started on the Every Member Canvass soon."

Timothy O'Dell was a conscientious pastor, a hard-working parish priest with a deep concern for his congregation. Every year he did his best with the canvass, but it wasn't one of his favorite tasks.

"Yes, I suppose we should," he replied. "Listen, why don't you call me this week and we can get together on it. In the meantime, maybe you could begin thinking about who we might get to be chairman this fall. I don't think George will do it again."

George Adams, a vestryman and one of the real leaders in the congregation, had been chairman of the canvass for the past three years. A junior executive in one of the local industries, George had taken the job three years ago when no one else would volunteer. In fact, for the past three years he had held the job by the same default. And he had done fairly well with it. Parish income had risen slightly, about 17 percent in those three years. It would have been more, but last year's campaign had been a disaster. As a gimmick, and at George's suggestion, they had tried to raise some extra money by selling stock in the church. Actually it was a fake stock sale. People had been asked to buy mythical shares in their church. "Invest in Christ's Church" had been their slogan. Investing didn't get you anything except a nicely done embossed stock certificate, certifying what you had pledged and granting you membership in what was to be called "Christ's Church Minutemen." The new Minutemen were to have a big dinner annually with an outside speaker, maybe a professional football player or local baseball hero. It sounded like a pretty good idea at the time George proposed it. And the vestry, eager every year for a new gimmick to light a fire under their canvass, accepted with enthusiasm. But, alas, as George's advertising friend, also a vestryman, had put it, "We ran it up the flagpole, but it just didn't fly." Pledges had come in as usual, a few increases, a few decreases, and the great majority of the pledges made out for the same as last year. Many of the stock certificates, passed out in church on Sunday when the canvass was finally completed, were left in the parish house after the coffee hour that day and in the pew racks in the church. Some were even found listlessly fluttering in the breeze in the parking lot.

A month or so later, when the rector had seen George at a meeting, the chairman had expressed his frustration. "I don't know what we can do about it. Everybody wants a good canvass, but nobody wants to help much," he had said. "Not raising the money we needed for the budget was bad enough. But it really bothered me this year, more than before, that our people just wouldn't work on it. I had trouble getting enough canvassers, and you hate to go back to the same people every year. Then the ones I did get to say yes didn't do what they were supposed to do. We planned to finish it up in two weeks, and it was two months before we got it cleaned up. I had to make the final twenty-five to thirty calls myself. At the end I was happy to have someone say, 'Put me down for the same as last year,' just to get them off my list. Personal income in this town has gone up on an average of 19 percent in the past two years while our parish income has gone up about 6 percent in the same time. It's really discouraging."

The junior executive had concluded by saying, "I'm sorry, Tim, but maybe you better find someone else to head it up next year."

Well, next year was here now, and, true to his word, the senior warden had called on Tuesday and the meeting with the rector was set for Thursday.

When Thursday had arrived, again, after the pleasantries had been exchanged, the senior warden began.

"Now, this year we have to come up with a really good gimmick to get people interested and excited about the canvass."

Introduction

In one of the *Peanuts* cartoons, Sally, Charlie Brown's friend, is pictured happily jumping rope. Suddenly she stops, looks around, and bursts out crying. Charlie Brown enters the scene to ask, "What 's the matter, Sally? What happened? Why are you crying?" To which Sally responds, "I don't know. I was jumping rope . . . everything was all right . . . when . . . I don't know. . . . Suddenly it all seemed so futile."

Perhaps "futile" is too strong a word to use about the feelings many churchpeople harbor about the stewardship task in our parishes. Better words might be

"frustrated"
"uneasy"
"confused"
"apprehensive."

Of all the things we do in the normal life of a parish church, few are approached with less educated enthusiasm and eager anticipation than is the annual spring or fall stewardship campaign. For many the need of raising money in the Church is viewed much as the Victorians viewed sex. It is necessary but not nice. In the past decade, innumerable articles and books have been written trying to suggest that there is no essential cleavage between the sacred and the secular, between the material and the spiritual. In spite of that, however, there still seem to be multitudes of Christians, clergy and lay people alike, who see the fund-raising task in the parish church as an unwelcome interruption in the ongoing spiritual life of the parish.

1

Attitudes range all the way from treating the stewardship campaign clearly as an interruption, a little like a commercial message in the middle of a good television program. It is separated from the program itself in sound, content, and appearance with no connection with what went before and what will come after. It is kept as short as possible so we can, as quickly as possible, get on with the real spiritual thing we are here to do.

Or, on the other extreme, it is so unwelcome that it is soft-pedaled and wrapped in such a series of religious clichés and spiritually sounding pieties as to go almost unnoticed.

There are obviously many exceptions to all this, situations in which conscientious clergy and lay people are facing their fund-raising task for what it is, an opportunity for people to grow spiritually by a proper use of and sharing of their possessions with God in God's world. But the feeling persists that these are the exceptions rather than the rule and that many of the faithful are still theologically and spiritually hung up when stewardship time comes around.

The very meaning of the word "stewardship" has gone through a significant shift in the past thirty years. Not so many years ago when the word stewardship was used, it meant, and it was understood to mean, the annual subtle or not so subtle effort to separate parish members from their money in the support of the parish budget. More recently, perhaps because the former seemed a little crass, the word stewardship began to take on a broader, more religious kind of definition. The United Stewardship Council, a little over thirty years ago, defined stewardship as:

> the practice of systematic and proportionate giving of time, abilities, and possessions, based upon the conviction that these are a trust from God, to be used in His service for the benefit of mankind.

In 1950 the Joint Department of Stewardship and Benevolence of the National Council of Churches succeeded the United Stewardship Council, and this same definition was accepted by them with an amendment that added the words "in grateful acknowledgement of Christ's redeeming love" at the end.

I have no quarrel with the definition. I endorse it wholeheartedly. But even this was not the end of the evolution. In the past decade, and especially in the past five years, an even broader understanding of stewardship has emerged. Stewardship, and more specifically Christian stewardship, has come to mean:

"what we do with what we have all of the time."

We have come to see, and quite correctly, that Christian stewardship involves all persons in their relationship with God, involving the whole person, relating the whole of our lives to our environment, to other people around us and, thus, fundamentally, to our God. Stewardship relates, we are learning, to how and in what ways we use everything God has given us. It includes our use of this created world and the space around it, life itself, our time, our skills, our relationships to people and things and, incidentally, our use of our possessions. It seems to me that therein lie the seeds of a serious stewardship problem. This broader definition is very helpful and useful, but with it, perhaps subconsciously, the idea has also grown that it is somehow more spiritually worthy to talk about our stewardship of the earth, now called ecology; or our stewardship of relationships, now called interpersonal dynamics; than it is to talk plainly and give it the same spiritual conviction and enthusiasm, of the stewardship of our material possessions, the stewardship of money. Indeed, there are clergy who will not speak of the latter at all, preferring to turn the annual stewardship sermon (the money sermon, in plain language) over to a layman or a visiting speaker. Their preference, I suspect, stems only in small part from their real or imagined inability to speak on the subject. Much more evidently, it seems to stem from the minister's belief that such a subject is just not quite proper for a minister in a Christian pulpit. When, out of necessity, ministers must address themselves to the subject, it is without much enthusiasm for the task.

Our stewardship campaigns themselves often betray the same misunderstanding. In one parish I served the term "Every Member Canvass" was abandoned and changed to "Every Member Visitation." While there was merit in the change, it was motivated primarily to change the campaign's image away from the raising of money toward a broader concern for the visiting of our membership. But significantly, in actual practice the change was in image only to soften the direct appeal for funds, because a direct appeal for funds was deemed not quite worthy of the Christian Church.

Or again, so often we see campaigns run in an attempt to seek pledges of time and talent in addition to pledges of money. Sometimes these are very well done and extremely helpful both to parish families who can offer time and talent more easily than money and to the parish as an institution which can use these gifts only too well. However, it can seriously be wondered if, in some cases, this combination kind of canvass is not in fact motivated by the underlying belief that adding the canvass for time and talent somehow makes the canvass for money in the Church more legitimate, a spiritual legitimacy which, in our minds, it doesn't quite seem to have on its own merit.

The purpose of this book is to suggest another way of looking at the stewardship in parish life. What follows is based on several convictions.

1) The relationship of people and their money is fundamentally a spiritual matter, as fraught with implications and potential for our spiritual life as is our life of prayer or our offering of time and talent to God in service to God's people. A writer of historical biography once wrote, "Show me where a man spends his money and I will show you the real man." Jesus, in the familiar words of Matthew 6:21, is quoted as saying, "Where your treasure is, there will your heart be also."

Both quotations suggest the same thing. Somehow, in some way, what people do with their money, how they think about it, where they spend it, what they will do to earn it, and the things to which they will give it, are some of the real clues to who they are inside, to what is essentially important to them, to what is really in their hearts. It is significant to note the order of things in the words of Jesus. He does not say, where your heart is there will your treasure be also. To be sure, genuinely convinced Christians are very likely to express their conviction, their enthusiasm for Jesus Christ in the way they think about and give of their money. Really turned-on parishes—congregations with a genuine, enthusiastic commitment to Christ—seldom have financial problems. But what Jesus is saying in Matthew's Gospel is that it also works the other way around. Create the atmosphere in which persons can give of their treasure in a conscientious, committed, spiritually oriented manner, and their giving may become the channel, the vehicle through which their enthusiasm and commitment to Jesus Christ will grow and deepen and blossom. If you doubt that, you might try an experiment. Go out and buy a few shares of stock in a legitimate business. Make it enough so that your financial stake is important to you. Then notice what part of the newspaper you turn to first when you pick it up. Unless you are a big investor dealing with these matters daily, I'd be willing to bet that three days out of four it will be to the financial page to check on your investment. Interest and enthusiasm follow money. "Where your treasure is, there will your heart be also."

Another way to say the same thing is to say that where we, in fact, make our most serious financial investments, where we determine we will spend and/or conscientiously give of our money, are the places where our real self, our inner self, is going to be most involved, most teachable, most responsive, and most open. To deal with persons in terms of what they do with their money is to deal with most people where they really live. To touch people effectively in an area of their real interest and concern, as we can do in a properly conceived stewardship effort in the church, can thus be to open for these same people an avenue to genuine spiritual growth, seldom open to us in any other way. Good stewardship has that potential. That, I believe, is something of what Jesus meant when he said, "Where your treasure is, there will your heart be also."

2) It is, therefore, extremely important that we build a proper and sound theological base for our stewardship efforts.

A *Peanuts* cartoon provides an illustration of what we are saying. Lucy and Linus are in the house looking out the window in a heavy rain storm. Lucy says, "Boy, look at it rain. What if it floods the whole world?" To which Linus replies, "It will never do that. In the ninth chapter of Genesis God promised Noah that would never happen again, and the sign of the promise is the rainbow." Lucy is reassured and smiles, saying, "You've taken a great load off my mind." To which Linus replies, "Sound theology has a way of doing that." The basic questions of life will ultimately be satisfied only by theological answers. This includes questions about money and our use of it.

A sound theology of money has a way of lifting the stewardship problem off our minds, making it a joy rather than a burden. But, more importantly, it has the potential to tap the spiritual roots of Christians at a point where they are the most teachable because it is here that they are the most concerned. A well-conceived, theologically sound stewardship program can be the most exciting spiritual adventure you can undertake in parish life. If there is a primary thesis that runs through this book, this statement summarizes it as well as any.

3) A person, indeed, a whole parish, can and should be enabled to grow spiritually in the life of grace and awareness of God through stewardship as much as in any other way. It has been said, "If you want to know about people's religion, don't ask them how they feel about Jesus Christ; ask them how they feel about their property."

Much is said from the pulpit, in Bible study groups, and in informal conversations among church people about the concepts of God's grace, God's love, God's providence, all given freely to us. These concepts are among the most powerful themes in the Church. But more often than not, delivered in a religious context, these great facts fall into a huge spiritual vacuum and are neither fully understood nor readily acted upon by church members.

A number of efforts have been made to measure the religious literacy of the typical Christian congregation. One such effort revealed the following: A simple sixth-grade test on Bible content was administered to an entering class of freshmen in a church-related college. Most of the students came from active church families. Out of fifty questions on which sixth-graders were supposed to score forty or above correct, the college freshmen averaged just under fourteen correct and the grades ranged as low as three out of fifty correct. Most didn't know what an epistle was, none could name all twelve of the apostles, and only thirty-three out of the almost 400 entering students could accurately describe what a parable was.

In another experiment I conducted in three different parishes the results were similarly disappointing. Some years ago the National Council of Churches produced a multiple-choice instrument testing the knowledge of church people on the nature of God, the uniqueness of Jesus Christ, the nature of the Sacraments, and the nature and authority of the Bible, among other items. The multiple choice answers were a variety of differing denominational points of view on these issues with a sprinkling of non-Christian views. In my use of the instrument with vestries and Bible study groups in these three parishes, of the fifteen items included, the attempt to identify the Episcopal view resulted in an average of five correct, with answers ranging all the way from one out of fifteen correct up to fourteen our of fifteen correct. But the weight was clearly to the lower scores.

These test results are not untypical of the results of many other like testing experiments done in the Church. The fact is that, with precious few exceptions, the average church member who worships on Sunday morning in a typical church is religiously and spiritually illiterate and massively inarticulate. It should not surprise us then that when the profound concepts of the grace and love and providence of God are talked about in church, the response of most listeners is one of appropriate respect because the words are familiar but also one of little understanding and equally little appreciation and acceptance.

I don't want to overstate the case and suggest that a proper theology of money will suddenly make these great themes abundantly clear and understandable. I do want to say that it is possible that when we connect the ideas of God's love and providence and grace to something real in a person's experience, to something he or she lives with daily, the concepts are more likely to come alive, become understandable and even appealing, to the point where the person is enabled to entertain them as true, begin to live with them and even grow in grace with them. What more real experience do most of us live with daily than our concern about and interest in our money. The struggle for financial security, a reasonable share of this world's goods and all that implies of plain survival, status, comfort, and the ability to do some of the things we want to do, are a real part of our daily thoughts, aspirations, ambitions, and sometimes even our prayers. To enable a person to see these things as related to God's grace, God's providence, and God's love is, at least potentially, to enable that person to see with new eyes what these powerful facts can mean in his or her life and, therefore, to be enabled to grow in them toward God. The temptation to oversimplify and perhaps even overstate the point here is great. But experience suggests that it can and does happen.

What all this means in the daily round of stewardship is that the "why" and the "how" of our stewardship approach are as critical to the spiritual life of the parish and people in it as the number of dollars raised is critical to the financial and program support we need.

What follows is based on these fundamental convictions. It will be divided into three parts. The first will be an attempt to explore a biblical theology of money and its uses. The second part, in three chapters, will try to suggest some of the details of a well-conceived stewardship program. The third part is a collection of some concrete kinds of materials that could be used or adapted in a stewardship campaign itself.

So, if you are still with me, turn the page, and let's explore some theology together.

Chapter 1

A Foundation
on Which to Build

When the stock market crashed in 1929, a lot of people found life a very heavy burden. Some of them jumped out of windows. Some of them lost their power to make decisions. Others did equally desperate things to themselves and others. Why? Because their god had died.

Much more recently, one day I went shopping with my wife to buy a new winter coat. We were in the women's department of a large department store. While my wife shopped I sat in the corner watching the people as they browsed through the racks of clothes. One woman caught my eye, browsing as she was through the most expensive rack of pants suits in the store. She was well-dressed in the latest fashions (as far as I could tell) and projected the image of a relatively affluent housewife. The clerk who waited on her was showing her almost everything that was there, without much success. Then, without any warning, the shopper dropped the last item on the floor and, in a rage, began to berate the clerk, the store, the manufacturer and everyone else in sight about the outrageous prices being charged, the gouging of customers by monthly interest rates on charge accounts, and the scheming fashion designers who changed styles constantly and forced her to change wardrobes to keep up with them. The rage lasted a full three to four minutes without letup until finally she stomped away from the racks and was gone. I have never felt as sorry for a sales clerk as I did then. But why? Why the rage? My guess is that her god, money, had lost some of its power for her and was in danger of losing its ability to comfort her.

These are both extreme examples to be sure. But they do illustrate the depth to which money—the getting of it, the spending of it, and the status and security it seems to promise—has always preoccupied people's minds. I believe this is increasingly true in our own generation.

Ask yourself this question. In your scale of things that are important to you, in what place would you put having enough money to do what you want to do? If you think deeply enough and consider it honestly, the answer will give you a pretty good indication of what you think about yourself and what you think about the kind of world in which you live. The value you give to having an adequate supply of money, or the ability to earn it, is probably the most accurate clue you can find to the kind of satisfactions you want from life and what you believe it means to be fulfilled as a person.

Money, or the material things it will buy, has always held an important place in human society. Our possession of it, or lack of it, has always defined our ability to purchase goods and services. But for most of us, it also defines in significant measure the nature and limits of many of our personal relationships. Money is not only important for what it will buy, but for how it affects relationships between people, and relationships between people and their God.

I will never forget an experience I had one time in the early years of my ministry. It was in a small, struggling parish. In midsummer our water pipes sprang a leak. Nothing serious, but a steady leak outside the building. At our vestry meeting we had to decide what to do about it. Investigation had shown that the leak was on our property all right, but it came in the line at a place ahead of our water meter. It was on our property, and we were responsible for it, but it wasn't affecting our building, and it wasn't costing us anything. In the discussion it was obvious that the decision was going to be to do nothing about it until the city discovered it and fixed it with city funds. Meekly, I suggested that there might be a moral issue involved, that we had a responsibility at least to report it (which might mean we'd have to fix it at church expense). The response I got was to be told nicely but firmly that I could have my morals, and they would have theirs. But right now we were talking about money. Then everyone laughed, and the meeting went on to other things.

Now these were not immoral men, calloused to moral considerations. But when it involved money, in this case just the church's money, the true blue of moral certainty became the faded gray of moral compromise. The men didn't change. The fact that their money was involved changed them. I was too young then to challenge them about it, and maybe I really didn't want to. I thought no more about it. But I've never forgotten it.

We can add to that very simple experience a multitude of others where money has been a major factor, sometimes the controlling factor in human relationships. A thousand illustrations to suggest the point can be summed up in the often-quoted proverb, "Never borrow money from (or lend money to) a friend—or you will lose a friend." When money enters the picture relationships change. Such is the power of money.

Ever since money was developed in some form where it could be saved, the accumulation of money has been a genuine interest for most people and a consuming hunger in others. For a great many people, primary elements of personality are subtly, or not so subtly, wrapped up in the green and silver ribbons of cold cash, or that which represents cold cash. These include:

- Self-worth or lack of it
- Sense of personal power or lack of it
- Sense of status or lack of it
- Sense of success or lack of it
- Sense of internal satisfaction or lack of it
- Sense of standing in the community or lack of it
- Sense of standing in a job or lack of it
- Sense of power over other people or lack of it

Whatever its economic purpose, money and the ability to earn it and possess it came to be regarded very early in human history as one of the clearest measures of the worth of human beings. Little has happened in history to suggest that this measure has lost any of its appeal or power over human life in our own time.

It is surprising to many people to discover that Jesus understood, as well as anyone who ever lived, this deep and compelling potential for good or ill in the relationship of a person and his or her money. If one were to ask a variety of people to describe the subect Jesus talked about most, I suspect the answers would be such things as forgiveness, prayer, sacrifice, joy, peace, and the Kingdom of God. A careful reading of the New Testament, however, suggests another and perhaps surprising answer. The subject Jesus talked about most, as the New Testament records it, is the relationship of persons and their material possessions.

It has been established that fully one-sixth of all the words of Jesus in the New Testament are concerned with this one subject, over one-third of all Jesus' parables are devoted to it. The fact is that the subject Jesus talked about more than any other was the proper use of one's possessions. To him there was little else that could potentially deepen or destroy a person's relationship to God and to other persons than the way he or she earned, thought about, and used his or her material possessions.

Consider only a few such obvious references in the Scriptures as the parable of the rich man and Lazarus (Luke 16:19–31), which relates vividly and unequivocably to the responsibilities and potential dangers of the misuse of wealth; the parable of the rich farmer (Luke 12:15–21), relating to the temptations of greed; in the midst of the great collection of spiritual wisdom that is the Sermon on the Mount, the teaching of Jesus on freedom from worry about possessions (Matthew 6:19–34); and the story of the widow's mite (Mark 12:41–44), which relates to the spirit and motive of giving. And these are only a few of the many references that could be cited.

And Jesus was not alone in his concern. The Old Testament is heavy with references to the same subject. The prophet Amos speaks of how God's judgment will fall on those who selfishly earn and spend money and allow it to be valued ahead of their worship and before God (Amos 8:4–8). The writer of Deuteronomy, in a powerful passage that takes the form of a commandment, exhorts people to remember and to thank God as the source of their wealth (Deuteronomy 8:10–18). And throughout the Old Testament there are numerous references to tithing, not necessarily as a system of giving but as a way to be reminded that God is the source and giver of all wealth, to whom thanks are to be offered (Leviticus 14:22, 27:30–33, Malachi 3:6–12).

In all of this two things seem clear. Money, and what it represents to us, has been a major preoccupation of every generation as it is in ours. Jesus, and others of God's servants before him, understood that and tried to speak to it in many, many ways.

It is important for us, then, that to live in this world as religious people we must develop a clear understanding of the meaning of money—the theology of money, if you will. And as important as having a clearly thought out theology of money is making that theology clearly evident and understandable in the ways in which we, as the Church, approach the stewardship task with the people in the parish.

Yet, how badly some of us sometimes handle that task, year after year! There are almost as many approaches to stewardship as there are parishes and years in which the task is undertaken. But, with some variations, the approaches I have observed seem to break down into three major categories. I have to admit that I recognize these primarily because, at one time or another, I have used them all.

A. THE NUMBERS APPROACH

In this a parish sits down and calculates what it will need next year, in addition to what has been given this year, to carry out the church's work in that parish. For example, let's suppose in a given parish it seems a 17 percent increase will be needed next year. It's carefully worked out: The church property is in disrepair and will need some work; the hardworking rector simply must be given a raise (and simply raising the salary to keep up with inflation won't do); the Sunday School program needs a lift for new materials and/or a paid director; a program we are trying to do in the community is in need of extra support; the diocese is asking us for more money for next year; and inflation has taken its toll on the church budget as it has on the family budgets of its members. So, the message is communicated that, all told, we believe we can manage next year on about a 17 percent increase in our giving. Therefore, (whether this is said by implication or directly) if everyone would just raise their pledge for next year by 17 percent, we will make it fine. And thank you very much.

Perhaps that is overdrawn some, but in a thousand ways this is the message that is delivered and heard.

Now, I'd like to suggest that there are several things wrong with that message.

1. IT PUTS THE EMPHASIS IN THE WRONG PLACE

The Numbers Approach will always put the emphasis on the dollars the church needs rather than on the dollars out of which we can give, that is, the giver's income. To start with a budget, whether it be last year's (to which a percentage increase has been applied) or next year's (which incorporates that increase), the center of attention remains on the numbers, on the balance sheet. You can talk all you like about program or ministries that the numbers will pay for, or giving out of income as a responsible Christian, but the natural tendency, I believe, is that few will hear what you say about ministry because many will be sharpening their mental pencils to go over the church's budgetary needs.

2. IT'S UNFAIR.

The basis of the message is that everyone is giving evenly, that parish family A and parish family B are already giving conscientiously in relation to their means and that a 17 percent increase from them both will continue to keep them conscientiously even. But the facts belie the assumption. While many families do give conscientiously, a great many more give, and will continue to give until challenged, far less than they could or should. To ask for a percentage increase, even by implication, puts an unfair burden on those who are doing their best to be faithful in their giving and allows the token givers to remain exactly where they are. Even if they respond to the percentage increase and give it, in all likelihood they will remain what they have been, token givers.

3. GENERALLY, THIS APPROACH REPRESENTS A MINIMUM RATHER THAN A MAXIMUM REQUEST.

It has been said that politics is the science of accomplishing what is reasonably possible. Politicians could take lessons from church vestries and finance committees. When the subject of next year's budget needs comes up, some important questions are given short consideration:

- What do we really want?
- What do we really want to do here?
- What things would we really like to do if money were not a problem?

They aren't asked because what occupies the mind is the single question,

- What can we reasonably expect to get?

Perhaps it is the fear of asking too much and facing failure that tempers us. Maybe it's just our reluctance to ask at all that frightens us. But, with the Numbers Approach, what we ask as an increase is pretty well informed by what we are fairly certain is attainable, or by how far short of our goal we can reasonably fall without getting hurt. Thus, the asking is generally calculated to meet a minimum standard of giving dictated by timidity rather than any maximum effort dictated by creative imagination about ministry and opportunity.

4. IT DOESN'T CHALLENGE ANYONE SPIRITUALLY.

One of the deepest concerns about much of the church fund raising we see is that we ask our people to give to the Church, or to a given parish, when what we need to ask them to do is to give to God. The effect of asking people to give to the Church is to base our appeal on the responsibility we can put on people for the parish to survive, on parish loyalties, on interest in parish activities, or even on loyalty to a particular parish priest. None of these are so much wrong or bad as they are incomplete. To base our appeal on these things is often to preclude any serious consideration of giving as a matter of a person's spiritual life, as a serious matter between a Christian and God.

We who are church people always operate on at least three levels in our spiritual life. We live on the level of denominational loyalty. That loyalty may be very strong or very weak, but one thing that holds us to the church is our denominational bonds. In addition to that, we live on the level of parish loyalty. To work in a particular parish, to give to a parish, is to be tied to an interest in seeing that parish survive, prosper and grow. Sometimes our parish and denominational loyalties are unbending, locking us into an attitude that is offended when things change. To see what is happening in the Church today and to see the response of many church members to what's happening is to see this locked-in attitude with crystal clarity. Beyond these loyalties, we also live on the level of a loyalty—a commitment—to God in Jesus Christ. Ideally, all three of these complement and reinforce each other. Realistically, however, one cannot help but observe that all too often the first two loyalties are used as a substitute for the third. We are so easily caught up in a kind of "Churchianity" that it shuts out the growth of our Christianity. Indeed, to be faithful to a church is a far easier commitment than to be faithful to Christ, or so it seems. When we deal with our stewardship task on the level of either denominational or parish commitments, we run the real risk of allowing these to be a substitute for any challenge to grow in relationship and commitment to God. Again, while we may *say* that our stewardship is a matter of the spirit, a matter between us and God, when the push really comes, it's the other necessities and other loyalties on which we are really banking. That's the real message church members will hear loud and clear and assume they are being asked to respond to.

B. THE "AREN'T YOU ASHAMED OF YOURSELF" APPROACH

Using this method, someone takes the trouble to find out where people are really spending their money. This will vary from place to place, but it can be rather precise if someone wants to be thorough. The message comes across something like this.

Someone has recently done a study on where people spend their money. And this is what they discovered. Nationally, we spend roughly:

$3 billion on cosmetics and personal care . . .

$3.5 billion on tobacco . . .

$10 billion on recreation and entertainment

$12 billion on alcoholic beverages (with their attendant headaches) . . .

$9 billion on jewelry, furs, gambling, and other luxuries . . .

(and here is the kicker)

$1.5 billion on churches and other charities of our choice.

What this means (we say) is that we care roughly:

2 times as much about our personal care than we do about God . . .

2½ times more about our cigarettes than we do about the Church . . .

8 times more about entertaining ourselves and our children than we do about providing our children with a religious education . . .

10 times more about drinking than we do about praying . . .

7 times more about our luxuries than we do about the Church's necessities . . .

And the climax of all that is the finger-pointing question, stated or implied, "Aren't you ashamed of yourself?"

The approach is summed up neatly in a little poem I clipped out of a parish newsletter not long ago. It was labeled "Quote of the Week," and was used during its Stewardship Drive.

Four thousand for my brand new car,
    Six thousand for a piece of sod,
Twelve thousand I paid to begin a house,
    A dollar I gave to God.

A tidy sum to entertain
    My friends in pointless chatter,
And when this world goes crazy mad,
    I ask, "Lord, what's the matter?"

Yet there is one big question
    For the answer I will search,
With things so bad in this old world,
    What's holding back my church?

Obviously, the great appeal of such an approach is that it is all too true. The priorities of most Americans are clear. From the point of view of religionists, they are somewhat, if not deeply, mixed up. The temptation to call that to the attention of the people and use that call as the base for additional giving is very great.

But there are some liabilities in the approach that beg to be pointed out.

1. IT APPEALS TO GUILT, OF WHICH PEOPLE HAVE TOO MUCH ALREADY, AND LAYS A HEAVIER BURDEN OF GUILT ON THEM.

If we are concerned in our stewardship solely with the raising of money, this approach might well satisfy our needs. Done right, it probably will shake a few extra dollars loose in the form of pledges from time to time. It will, because we all know that the facts are correct. Our priorities are not what they should be.

But if our intention in stewardship is to enable us to recognize the acts of God in our behalf and to enable us to make some deeper commitment to God through our giving, guilt and adding to that burden of guilt are surely an unworthy base for such growth. To be sure, our feelings of guilt sometimes do bring us to a kind of repentance that will change our priorities. But far more often, it is our very sense of guilt that drives us away from God.

I've never run a scientific survey of the real attitudes and feelings of church people. But my unscientific guess, based on nearly thirty years of parish ministry, is that one of our most deep-seated feelings is our almost universal and uneasy sense of unworthiness before God. Most Christians sense that, because of our plain sinfulness, somehow we must earn our way into God's favor. To be sure, there are many in our time who grandly and vigorously reject any idea of sin and sinfulness on their part. These will proclaim loudly and often that sin is obsolete, especially their own, and that what they seek and will find is acceptance for what they are and are in the process of becoming. But even their very bravado often betrays them. For underneath all the claims and rejections, I believe, many are not all that sure. Indeed, some are absolutely sure that they are not good enough, nor will they ever be. The very burden of guilt they already carry is the major source of their claims to be free of judgment. It is almost as though they desperately hope that, if they shout "freedom from guilt" loud enough, it just might come true. But as I view church people, whether they claim the obsolescence

of sin or not, this sense of unworthiness before God seems more
and more evident.

In a recent book titled *The Gospel in a Broken World,* John
Snow makes the same point in a different context.

> To say to the average American today that God loves him is
> probably to him the most preposterous statement that could be
> made . . . After all, he smokes, drinks, possibly uses drugs, swears,
> increasingly goofs off at work, has been or is sexually promiscu-
> ous (at least by God's standards), . . . and on occasion spends
> more than he earns. He is, by traditional standards, an object for
> cosmic punishment and not for God's love (p. 41).

Of course, the assertion of the Gospel we proclaim is that
human beings *are* the objects of God's love. The love and salvation of God in Christ are freely offered and freely given. The
Gospel does not demand that we meet some standard before we
can be loved and accepted by God. But that is a terribly difficult
message for most of us to hear and appropriate.

If in the stewardship task, we deny that message and instead
feed our sense of guilt and intensify it, what spiritual growth
can there be? We may shake a few billfolds a little harder, but
we also run the real risk of driving people away from the very
God we proclaim and worship.

2. CRITICISM FOR FAILURE SELDOM STIMULATES PEOPLE TO DO THEIR BEST.

Giving, be it to the Church or to any worthy cause, is not an
intellectual process but an emotional process. Most of our giving
is done because we have been motivated by our feelings, feelings which have been stirred by needs and truths that have been
presented to us in a way that we can understand them. Accusing
people of not giving what they ought to give puts them on the
defensive rather than motivating them to give more, responsibly. Child psychology has long since learned that behavior in
a child is modified by approval and acceptance far more readily

than by criticism. In the stewardship task we need to learn that same lesson. More will be said about this very big subject later.

C. THE "CRY POOR" APPROACH

In this, through both the written and spoken word, the message communicated seems to come out something like this.

> Friends, we are living in perilous times. For some years now our parish has been here on this corner serving and ministering to the needs of our people. But this year we are in grave danger. After years of distinguished ministry we have come to the crossroads. One road leads to further ministry; the other to a severe cutback in ministry. But, to continue to serve, there are some things we simply must do.

And here are listed all the desperate needs, which might include leaks in the roof, cracks in the parking lot surface, malfunction in the heating equipment requiring major repair, the need for secretarial help, janitorial help, a whole new Sunday School curriculum, etc. The climax is reached as the appeal is made.

> Unless we receive substantially increased pledges, we simply cannot do these necessary things for which we do not now have enough money.

Anyone reading this can elaborate from your experience to fill in the details. It all adds up to a message that says, "Poor old St. _____. Won't you all please dig a little deeper to help her out in this time of crisis?" Sometimes this message is delivered when the crisis is real enough. Sometimes the message is delivered when there is no crisis, or at least no crisis as perilous as is described. The theory, of course, is that very few people can resist such a plea from their own parish and will, indeed, respond to save the parish from a fate worse than death.

Clearly, nothing is wrong with a special appeal based on legitimate need, when that need is laid upon us. But as a regular diet, this approach seems to have some severe liabilities.

1. IT APPEALS TO FAILURE
INSTEAD OF EFFECTIVE SUCCESS.

If there is a single principle in modern advertising that runs through almost every ad, it is the principle that success begets success, failure begets failure. The proud claims of a great variety of businesses advertising today are all claims of success. One hamburger vendor claims that "10 billion have already been sold." Another claims having assets of "X millions of dollars and going up." Another claims to have so and so, the professional football (baseball, hockey) player as a customer. All this is done to present a picture of success that will attract new customers. The premise is that people want to be associated with successful things and will spend (or give) their money where success is already proven (or claimed). To cry poor in business is the death knell. In the Church it may work once but in the long run, this approach will lose you money, members, enthusiasm and interest.

2. IT TRIES TO MOTIVATE GIVING OUT OF PITY
INSTEAD OF THANKSGIVING.

I happen to believe in the Church and the God of the Church. Most of all, I believe in the actual worth and the tremendous potential worth of the parish church as the setting where God-person, and person-person spiritual encounters can take place and be fostered. The parish church, while it is sometimes magnificently ineffective and dull, will nonetheless never become effective and alive from pity. Indeed, pity for the old church is an unworthy motive to sustain any effective stewardship, or anything else for that matter, including any real spiritual growth in and through our giving.

ANOTHER APPROACH

Now, to be sure, some of what has been said in the paragraphs above is overdrawn and stereotyped, but perhaps it makes a point. In any case, it does lead us to consider another way of thinking about our stewardship, a way that can be shown to be more theologically and biblically sound and much more spiritually challenging to church people. Experience clearly shows that it will also provide greater participation and better feeling on the part of church people. Incidentally, it will provide a more adequate financial response as well. And it requires that we go back into Scripture for our background.

We have said earlier that the Bible is full of references to the relationship of human beings to their material possessions. What are some of these and what do they say?

The book of Genesis begins with the words:

In the beginning God created the heavens and the earth.

The theme of God's ownership, through creating, and human trusteeship (stewardship of the earth and what is in it) sounded here in the first verses of Genesis, is a recurring biblical theme in both the Old and New Testaments. The writer of Deuteronomy (Deuteronomy 8:10–18) picks up the theme, when, after listing many human accomplishments, such as building houses, the raising of herds and flocks, and the accumulation of money, he then warns his readers that the temptation to consider those things as their own will be great.

Beware lest you say in your heart, "My power, and the might of my hand has given me this wealth."

And the Deuteronomic writer lays it out clearly.

You shall remember the Lord your God, for it is he who gives you power to get wealth. (Deuteronomy 8:18)

God is the source, and humanity is the recipient and user of God's gifts. The book of the Chronicles strikes the same theme again. David, near the end of his reign, has proclaimed a day of offering for the Temple of God. The initial offerings to God are from David's own hand. And then the text goes on at length to describe how the head of every household in the land came forward and made their freewill offerings. The climax of the incident is reached when the offering is concluded, and David addresses this prayer to God.

> But who am I, and what is my people, that we should be able thus to offer willingly? For all things come from thee, and of thy own have we given thee. . . . O Lord our God, all this abundance that we have provided for building thee a house for thy holy name comes from thy hand and is thy own. (I Chronicles 29:1–16)

Again, in a more indirect way, the same theme is caught by the prophet Malachi. In severe words of judgment, Malachi, speaking for God, chastises the people for withholding their offerings from God, calling it robbery. The emphasis on the tithe here is less important, in my view, than the principle that provokes it, God's ownership of all things and human trusteeship.

Turning to the New Testament and, for most of us, more familiar territory, the same basic principle is sounded again. In three parables especially, Jesus uses this theme of God's ownership and our trusteeship. In the parable of the talents (Matthew 25:14–30), Jesus is saying that whatever we possess (it matters not whether we interpret talents to mean money, as in the parable, or skills, opportunities, creative talents, education, or even life itself), we possess because it has been given by God's hand. And from the gift, some return to God is expected. (And again it matters not whether we see the expected return in terms of a consecrated life, service to our fellow human beings, or offerings of our money that these gifts have produced). The point of the parable is God's ownership and humanity's trusteeship.

Another parable puts it equally well, the parable of the tenants (Mark 12:1–12). In this parable, while the major theme has to do with the rejection of God's Son by the Jews, nonetheless, underlying that theme is the assumption that what human beings have, they have because it has been given to them at the hands of God. And, from the gift, a return is expected.

Yet a third parable suggests a similar theme. The parable of the laborers in the vineyard (Matthew 20:1–16) clearly describes the proposition that God is a giver of gifts and that God's gifts exceed anything we can do to earn them. The poignancy of the words of the parable, "Am I not allowed to do what I choose with what belongs to me?" put in the mouth of God, is a proclamation of the depth out of which God desires to give "of what belongs to me" (note the emphasis on God's ownership) to his people.

There are other references that can be made. But these suffice to suggest that a theology of money, a theology of what we possess, begins with the principle that what we have, we have been given. The source of these gifts is a God who loves us and wants the best for us.

Now, let's try to be a little more precise about it. When we speak of God's ownership and humanity's trusteeship, how do we translate that from the Scripture to the world in which we live? There are many ways to illustrate it, but I have used three illustrations that make sense to me and seem to be understandable to others. The first comes from the world of agriculture.

Not so many years ago, the Associated Press released a study done by an agricultural school in Iowa. It reported that production of 100 bushels of corn from one acre of land, in addition to the many hours of the farmer's labor, required 4,000,000 pounds of water, 6,800 pounds of oxygen, 5,200 pounds of carbon, 160 pounds of nitrogen, 125 pounds of potassium, 75 pounds of yellow sulphur, and other elements too numerous to list. And, in addition to these things, which no human being can produce, rain and sunshine at the right time are critical. Human beings have no control over these things. It was estimated, the report went on to say, that only 5% of the produce of a farm can be attributed to human efforts. Indeed, the earth is the Lord's, and we are the recipients of great gifts.

Another illustration of the same point, much more simply and directly made, is a homely four-line poem.

> Back of the loaf is the snowy flour,
>   And back of the flour, the mill.
> And back of the mill are the
>   wheat and the showers,
> And the Sun and the Father's will.

Indeed, "All things come of thee, O Lord."

A third illustration that again makes the same point, comes from a lawyer's office.

Some years ago a Louisiana law firm was asked to undertake a title search for some property in New Orleans. They successfully traced the title back to the Louisiana Purchase in 1803. But their clients were not satisfied with that. So the search went on. Finally, the law firm sent the following letter to their clients.

> Gentlemen:
>   Please be advised that in the year 1803, the United States of America acquired the territory of Louisiana from the Republic of France, by purchase. The Republic of France, in turn, acquired title from the Spanish Crown by conquest; the Spanish Crown having obtained it by virtue of the discoveries of one Christopher Columbus, who had been authorized to undertake his voyage by Isabella, Queen of Spain, who obtained sanction for the journey from the Pope, the Vicar of Christ, who is the Son and Heir of Almighty God, who made Louisiana.

What we are accustomed to call our own is not really ours. It is God's. What we do is to hold it for a time, use it, add to it and then pass it on. God is the owner. We are the trustees.

Now the illustrations are fine. They are understandable because, I believe, the vast majority of thoughtful people, when it is called to their attention, really do believe that they have been given bountiful gifts of God's hand.

But it is not quite as simple as that. In modern America, where the Protestant work ethic has had such a hold on us, where competition and pride of accomplishment are so deeply built into our economic life, there will be many who will argue that to some degree what they have, they have by their own sweat and hard work. Some will argue the point with fierceness born out of genuine pride. For some, their pride of accomplishment, economically, is a very large part of their ego support system. A good illustration of this is seen in the attitude of a great many hard-working people in our time about the so-called welfare mother. The woman is often enough and physically fit enough to work. But she stays home with her children and is supported by public assistance. It has been said by some, and is believed by many, many more, that these mothers should get about supporting themselves. "After all," they say, "no one is supporting me. I have to go out and earn it. And so should they." For some, the words are more refined than that. But what are they really saying? It is possible that behind the words are other words, words that have nothing to do with welfare mothers at all, but with themselves; words that are intended to say, "Look at me. Look at what I have done and at what I have by my own plain hard work." Of course, they are quite correct about what they have done. To say to them that what they have, they have because God has given it to them, is to say something, at best, only half believed. So we must go on and say more.

There is another homely illustration that helps to lead into the more we need to say. It goes like this.

A minister once went out to visit one of his parish members. He lived in a rundown house whose front yard had been left in a real tangle of weeds and brush and tall grass. But over a few months after he bought the place, the man had literally transformed that front yard into a beautiful lawn and garden. When the minister called he saw the wondrous improvement. He said to the man, "My, isn't it wonderful what you and God have been able to do with this yard?" The man thought for a moment and then replied, "Yes, it is, but you should have seen it when God had it alone."

The story has value because it points to the obvious truth that much of what we have, we have because we have worked for it, because we have been willing to invest our time and effort and enthusiasm and money to be where we are on the economic scale. It is out of a sharp awareness of their sweat and toil that many people claim pride of ownership, a pride of accomplishment, and so easily say, "Look at what I have done." There is no question that, for a great many hard-working people, this is the simple truth as far as it goes. We have what we have because we have worked very hard for it.

But to acknowledge that is not to deny the principle of God's ownership. Here biblical theology asks us to take one more step. It asks us to acknowledge that what we have done, we have done because we have been the recipients of countless gifts. A life to live; we didn't earn that. A brain with which to think, a talent to use; these things we have not earned. The raw materials of the earth with which to create, a body with which to work, and countless opportunities in which to grow, learn, mature, and develop as people. These are not earned. These are given. While we may vary tremendously in what each of us will make of these gifts, basically and undeniably they are gifts given, for which more of us may then reach the point of being able to say, "Look what I have done with what God has given me." Indeed, we may even be enabled to come to the point of being able to say, "Isn't that something of what life is about, to take what we have been given, both in ourselves, and other people and in the earth; to use it, to develop it, and from it to produce something of value, something of beauty in this world?" That something may be a product, a service, a better person, or a deeper relationship. But this understanding is possible only when we acknowledge that God is the owner and we are the trustees.

It seems to me that any coherent theology of money—the earning, spending, and giving of it—must begin with this.

This principle is expanded for a Christian in one magnificent way. The greatest gift of God to us has been the gift of his Son,

Jesus Christ, and, through him, the opportunity to live in the power of the Holy Spirit. Clearly, when we have thought about the gifts of the earth, life and the human qualities of body, brain, talents, and the like, and identified these as gifts of God, we have only scratched the surface. As Christians we must go on and speak of what Paul calls "the unspeakable riches of Christ" (Ephesians 3:8). Each reader will want to develop his or her own Christology. That is not our purpose here. But no discussion of God's gifts can ever be completed without some reference to the great (and wholly undeserved) gifts of:

> An avenue of prayer available in the name of
> Christ Jesus,
>
> The possibility of forgiveness through the
> intercession of Christ Jesus,
>
> The assurance of salvation through the merits
> of Christ Jesus,
>
> A life after death through the resurrection of
> Christ Jesus,
>
> And, a power to have and live a life abundant
> through living, in Paul's phrase, "in
> Christ Jesus."

Beyond this direct bounty, we have, as all persons do, the possibility of the life of joy in the power of the Holy Spirit. Without detailing these things—for you can interpret for yourself what they mean to you—the point I am trying to make here is that we are the recipients of almost limitless gifts with which to live, in which to grow, and by which we have much of what we possess and tend to call our own.

Now, what has all this to do with our giving? It is my belief that all this sets the motive for giving, a motive which is at once biblically sound and fundamentally appealing. We give because that is one way we have of directly expressing our thanksgiving to God for these gifts. The purest of motives for giving is to give because we have been given to. Giving can be our thankful response to God who has given to us.

As critical as it is to say that, it is equally critical to note what that kind of motive does to (or for) the giver. To ask people to give out of thanksgiving is to ask them to relate creatively with their God and not to a parish budget. It asks them to respond out of what they have, i.e., their income, rather than to the needs of the Church. This makes their giving a matter of their spiritual life rather than a matter of parish survival. It asks a person to be a Christian with his or her money and not just a fund raiser and/or a budget supporter.

So, all in all, what have we said? We have tried to make four points:

1) Money, the earning of it and the spending of it, has always been one of the major preoccupations of people in all ages, including our own.

2) Jesus, and the prophets before him, understood the implications of this better than we do and, over and over again, spoke to the potential spiritual good or ill that rises out of our relationship to our money.

3) The message of both Old and New Testaments about our money is the powerful but simple reminder that God is the owner and the bountiful giver of both our material and spiritual wealth, and we are recipients of these great gifts.

4) In the recognition and acceptance of this basic fact, we can understand and come into a relationship with this God of grace and providence and love through our giving, motivated by our thanksgiving for these overwhelming gifts at God's hands.

It seems, at least to me, that a foundation built in principles at least akin to these I have suggested is not only desirable but essential to any stewardship effort we may undertake, if our stewardship is to be more than simply an effort to raise money. Indeed, built on such a foundation, our considerations of stewardship can then open up the genuine possibilities of spiritual growth, both in the life of the individual Christian and in the life of the parish as a whole.

Chapter 2

But What About
Program and Budget?

In the last chapter we tried to take a look at our theological and biblical foundations. We tried to suggest that giving is really a matter between a person and God. God is the giver, and people give as one way they can respond to God out of thanksgiving for the gifts they have received at God's hands.

How, then, does all that relate to our need to support a parish program and budget? More practically, what does all that say to the manner in which programs and budgets can best be presented in a stewardship campaign.

Before we take a specific look at that question, there are two clear implications in what we are saying that need to be examined and understood.

1. *If Christian stewardship, in our context, is anchored in the relationship of people and their money, then Christian stewardship will relate to one's income, how one earns it, how one spends it, and how and if one decides to return a portion of it to God who is the ultimate source of it.* It does not relate to the Church's program or budget needs. The focus of stewardship is the effect the use of our money has on our relationship to God. To base our stewardship approach on the Church's budget and program, therefore, is to shift the focus and, indeed, to allow it to get in the way of that larger consideration.

Some years ago the stewardship committee of a parish I served was wrestling with plans for the coming fall canvass. Most of the questions we were dealing with were questions of program and budget adjustments we were going to have to make. We seemed to be getting nowhere as we tried to incorporate these needs into a theme for our canvass. Finally, after two hours of frustration, I suggested we break for the night. Then I asked the committee to take home an assignment. "We seem to be hung up on what the Church needs and how much we think we can raise," I ventured. "So, would you go home and, for the next meeting, write a brief answer to this question: 'Why should anyone give anything at all to the Church?' Bring your answers back next week." The answers that came back were all essentially the same—and a surprise to almost everyone on the committee. One report that summarizes much of what was written is worth quoting in part. It came from a businessman who works in a highly competitive field.

> Why should anyone give anything at all to the Church? I can only speak for myself. But for myself the answer is that I have been fortunate, blessed in many aspects of my life, including my business, and I want to share this fortune with others. I don't think I feel guilty about all this good fortune, but I have come to realize that by no means have I been completely responsible for it, materially or otherwise. If this is so, then is it really mine to do with it as I please? No, not really. I feel responsible to the source of these blessings and want to do the "right thing" with them. And, as time has gone by, I've come to feel that these things are less and less my own doing. At the same time, I've begun more and more to realize where they did come from— God. And the "right thing" has come more and more to mean what I think God would want me to do with my blessings. And one of the important "right things" is giving or sharing them with others.

Note some things about this response. It makes no reference to program and budget and the obvious need we faced to support them. But it puts the emphasis in the right place: (1) on the need to return to God out of thanksgiving, and (2) on basic income as the most immediately tangible measure of God's blessings and as the focus out of which our giving has to come. But significantly, neither of these ideas was seriously considered by the committee until questions of program and budget had been put aside.

2. *It follows, then, that the stewardship campaign needs to be conducted prior to the formation of the parish budget.* The stewardship questions ought never to be, "How much do we need?" or even the better question, "What programs can I help support?" The basic question needs to be, "What do I have out of which I can conscientiously return, as a Christian, to God?" Our need is to give to God and not to a budget and to give to God through many channels, of which the Church is only one. But basically, when we pledge to the Church we are giving, and need to know we are giving, to God and not the Church.

Another man on the same stewardship committee, an accountant who works as a corporation business manager, put his finger on it.

> I want to give him something in return, even though I could never begin to repay him for all these blessings. How can *I give* anything to God? I can't touch him. I can't see him. But I can give to help others become more aware of his love for them. I can do this by giving to my church, by giving gladly, even happily, *because the gift is for him*, who has given me so much.

To talk budget and program to these people and to try to invent slogans to make that budget and program come alive, as we had tried to do for one whole night, was to miss the whole center of their motive to give. The budget and program just got in the way of their *Christian response* in giving. I suspect that there are many others who, while they may not say it the same way, feel the same thing. Even some in our parishes who are often preoccupied with budgets may be so, consciously or otherwise, as a way to avoid any demanding considerations of a more Christian giving response.

So the appeal needs to be directed toward a person's income, not the parish's need. Parish budgets need to be considered only after the stewardship campaign is completed.

But these two preliminary comments still leave us with the question, How, then, do we present program needs at stewardship time? Perhaps the distinctions I'm about to make will seem like drawing a fine line. But I believe them to be the difference of day and night.

1. PRESENT PRESENT PROGRAM NEEDS IN TERMS OF THE CHALLENGE AND OPPORTUNITY TO MINISTRY.

People are seldom motivated to give to the Church as a church. They tend to want to give money to the Church (and to other charities as well) in order that the Church may minister, that is, that the Gospel may be preached, the sick visited, the bereaved comforted, the children taught the story of Christ, the adults enabled to learn and grow—and that the ministry of the Church may be taken from the building into the neighborhood, the diocese, the nation, the world.

Such presentations of ministry should not be labeled with price tags. In fact, they probably will not follow the line-by-line budget items you will later construct. What they constitute really is a parade of people and facilities, paid professionals and volunteers alike, who are doing things, saying things, ministering to the needs of the world and the people in it, in the name of Jesus Christ. The story of that ministry is told by people who are given flesh and blood and not by a set of figures in a column.

In other words, a dry presentation of figures or percentages of increased dollars that are needed, even if the need is described in terms of things to be done, is basically devoid of any appeal to the imagination. But to describe the work, to describe the opportunities, to describe the ministry that goes on, without the encumbrance of dollar signs, will enable people to put clothes and shoes and hands on their giving, bringing immense enjoyment and satisfaction to the giver.

Many parishes have already moved in this direction by organizing their actual post-canvass budgets into "ministries."

While there are many ways it can be done, budget items could be listed in this fashion, for example:

- "The Ministry of Our Hands," which contains salaries and benefits for paid people . . .
- "The Ministry of Our Feet," which contains money given to work outside the parish . . .
- "The Ministry of Our Minds," which contains all educational work . . .
- "The Ministry of Our Voices," which contains the music program . . .
- "The Ministry of Our Hearts," which contains items of parish and inter-parish social-fellowship life . . .
- "The Ministry of Our Arms," which contains administration . . .
- "The Ministry of Our Muscles," for the housekeeping, janitorial items . . .

These are not the only categories available. They might have the advantage, if thought through carefully, of being tied together with Paul's phrase in I Corinthians 12:27, "Now you [plural, meaning the gathered Corinthian church] are the body of Christ and individually members of it." A parish is the body of Christ, so why not a budget designed in terms of the ministries of our various parts? But whether this or some other way is devised, the point to be made is that program presentations need to be made incarnate, if I may use that word, given flesh and populated with people who do things, both in and out of the parish. Just picture in your mind the difference in appeal between picking up a budget that lists items like:

Salary   _____
Car Allowance   _____
Pension   _____
Sunday School   _____
Property Maintenance   _____
Etc.   _____

and one that lists items like (to use a different set than the ones suggested above):

To minister to the human
needs of our congregation
(includes costs of salaries,   _____
etc. of clergy)

To minister to human need
outside the parish   _____
(includes cost of all
outreach, missionary
programs)

To keep God's house decently
and in order (property   _____
maintenance, etc.)

To sing the praises of God   _____
(music program)

To deepen knowledge and faith
among us (educational   _____
program)

Etc.   _____

The one tends to be dry, dull, and boring. The other has people in it, doing things, and has the potential to come alive in terms of things that are being done, and/or could be done, in and through the parish.

This is not to say that there is any magic in simply reorganizing the budget figures under a different set of titles, although I believe that's a good thing to do. What I'm trying to suggest is that things that are done, or could be done, in ministry have life when they can be seen as ministry and not just as dollars that need to be spent. In such a presentation, prior to an Every Member Canvass, the cost of such ministries should not be talked about. It is the tasks that can be done, the help that can be offered, the word that can be spoken, the contact that can be made, that captures the enthusiasm of people. The financial support of such ministries will need to be talked about later when your pledging is done and budget preparation time has arrived.

2. DREAM SOME DREAMS WITH YOUR CONGREGATION.

So often in program presentations at canvass time, even well-done presentations, we concentrate on things we want to do next year. While they may be urgent, the missing element is the far-out dream we may have. "What are we moving toward five years from now?" "Where are we going or where could we go in this parish if we had the courage and the funds three years or five years or even ten years from now?" One parish rector based one of his stewardship sermons on the theme "If I Had a Million Dollars." It was based on an old television series called "The Millionaire," in which a million dollars was given to a series of people as a gift. Each program then dealt with how they reacted and used that sudden wealth. His sermon asked the question, "What would we do with one million dollars if we had it in this parish?" Then he began to dream of things and happenings and ministries that might open up for that parish. He didn't get any million-dollar gifts, but he did open up the minds and the imaginations of the people to see what their tight budget had never allowed them to see, the possibilities there might be for that parish in the years ahead. People want to know, and really get turned on when they do know, that some-one is looking ahead down the road, dreaming dreams of what *might* be. Most people want to be a part of a dream, if that dream will serve the needs of people and is reasonably possible of fulfillment. And surely, it is only as we dream a little that these dreams may become reality.

3. INCLUDE IN ANY PROGRAM PRESENTATION A FULL SHARE OF SPACE AND IMAGINATION TO PROGRAMS OUTSIDE THE PARISH.

Parochialism is an insidious disease in the Church. It is never more insidious than when it invades our stewardship efforts. As the individual giver shares of his or her income with God through the Church, so the Church shares of its income outside of itself. The ministry that goes on outside the parish needs clothes to wear in people's minds perhaps more than that which goes on inside the parish because it is so much less visible. The fact that much of the so-called missionary giving of many parishes nowadays is through agencies and boards, and, therefore, relatively anonymous to the giver, makes the problem even more urgent. I do not wish to return to the days where outside program people and missionaries needed to appear before us to plead for support. But there is a great need to personalize and visualize the ministries being undertaken in God's name everywhere. To lose sight of this or minimize it at stewardship time is to miss a whole exciting, appealing and, I believe, necessary dimension of ministry in our world.

There is another dimension to this problem.

It is one of the hardest lessons we need to learn. To shut out or minimize giving to legitimate causes outside the parish has the effect of minimizing giving to parish programs as well. To present opportunities for support of work outside the parish has the effect of broadening the base of parish support as well.

George Lundy of Marts and Lundy, Inc., a New York–based firm providing consulting services to charitable and non-profit organizations in fund raising, has written of this in the introduction of a book titled *Successful Fund Raising Sermons*.

> I can't understand the ministers or the official boards of our churches who take the position that they will not allow their members to be solicited for outside enterprises. I suspect that it is because many of them are fearful that money given to enterprises outside of the church is bound to decrease the amount the

church would have available for its own work. How wrong they are! I suspect this is because they do not understand another aspect of giving. It is not only an emotional thing, but it becomes a habitual thing; repeated giving develops "giving habit tracks" . . . which makes it easier to do again. Giving makes it easier to give again, and the people who have developed a habit of giving are those who are inclined to give additional sums and who get greater satisfaction out of it. The churches which recognize this fact and see to it that other causes outside the church itself such as colleges, hospitals, missions, etc., are given the opportunity to present their needs to its members are always the churches that find their own finances easiest. If I were pastor of a church I would see to it that every year the members of my church were given an opportunity to participate in these enterprises . . . knowing the result would be more funds for my own work than I could possibly hope to have otherwise. (pp. 10, 11).

4. MAKE YOUR PROGRAM PRESENTATION VISUAL AS WELL AS VERBAL.

It's an old but true cliché: a good picture is worth a thousand words. And good pictures are not that hard to come by. The ministry in and out of the church can be dramatized by a series of posters simply but well done, by collages done out of magazine pictures and printed words, by actual photographs blown up of the parish in action, by slides, by transparencies, and by other means. Indeed, by a multitude of visual aids the parish program can be given wings on which to fly into the imaginations of the people.

One parish priest told me that for a year someone had taken photographic slides of virtually every aspect of the parish life, some posed, some candid. To these were added some slides of work outside the parish in which the parish had an interest. With a tape recorder and three screens, a synchronized multimedia presentation was prepared for use at stewardship time. The emphasis of the presentation was to say, "This is what we can do with the gifts you give to God through this parish." The effect was to create a real and new excitement about ministry in that parish and a genuinely new enthusiasm for being a part of it. Incidentally, it also resulted in a 25 percent increase in giving to God through that parish.

You don't have to be an artist or an expert to do these kinds of things. A search of your congregation will probably turn up several someones who have both the skills and the interest to get it done. And that's a kind of stewardship all of its own.

5. *POPULATE YOUR PRESENTATION OF MINISTRY WITH FAMILIAR PEOPLE AND PLACES.*

Nothing will provoke interest and make ministry come alive as quickly as seeing pictures of familiar people engaged in it. The faces of clergy and parish people (adults and children alike) bring a kind of built-in reality and urgency to your descriptions that is appealing and dramatic. Familiar people clothe ideas and programs with flesh and blood that brings them right down to home for the viewer. Familiar places where ministry takes place (the church building, local hospitals, rest homes, the diocesan headquarters, and neighborhood places into which your ministry is reaching) all have the same appealing impact. In the context of seeing these familiar people and places, unfamiliar people and places also take on a reality they might not otherwise have. It is as though you are saying, "In addition to these familiar people and places, our ministry reaches out where we have never been in person." Then the unfamiliar look of people and places, in other neighborhoods, the diocese, the world, take on a substance and form less romantic and more solid and believable. All such pictures, whether familiar or not, have more impact when the people are doing something connected with ministry and not just standing still, smiling.

6. BE COMPLETE, BUT BE HONEST ABOUT WHAT IS REALLY HAPPENING.

You are not selling something as much as you are teaching something about the life of the parish ministry. The task is not to overstate the wonderful things that are happening in order to coax more dollars from people, but to inspire interest in the value and variety of ministry to provoke insight and commitment. There is value, therefore, in illustrating failures as well as successes. To say, by word and picture, "We tried this but it didn't work out . . . but we did try and will continue to try other things," delivers the message of the continual search for ways to minister, a search that bespeaks life and vitality. Or to say, "Here is something we would like to do, where we see a need, and would like to see how we in this parish can help to meet it," is to say again that the ministry is vital and dynamic, on the growing edge of service to others. Say only what is honestly possible, or already happening. But variety and completeness teach and inspire credibility and will tend to provoke a more thoughtful and deeper response.

All of this might well be summed up by quoting George Lundy again.

> Speaking as a layman I would say to you as pastors: Do not hesitate to present to us all the causes of the Kingdom in such a way that we can feel that we are really having a part in carrying them on, and you will not be disappointed in the result. Present them to us graphically so that we may be able to visualize them; dramatize them so that we may more clearly understand the opportunity for service that they provide . . . and we will not fail you (Ibid, p. 11).

Chapter 3

Sacrificial Giving: A Biblical and Personal Perspective

The phrase "sacrificial giving" is commonly used in connection with financial stewardship programs in the Church. I have a hunch, backed by some experience in hearing and reading about how the words are used, that our theology of sacrifice is not as sound as it might be. Let your mind float for a moment over these words, "sacrificial giving." What images do they conjure up? For most, I suspect, the images are those of reaching down a little more, of giving up something we want or even treasure so we can dig a little deeper for the Lord and for the Church. To make a sacrifice, we often say, is to deny ourselves something for the sake of the nobility of our giving. Sometimes these words are accompanied by such slogans as "Give until it hurts," "Give until you can feel it," or, in a bit of verbal gymnastics, we say, "Give until it feels good." I would submit that this is to misunderstand sacrificial giving; to misunderstand the biblical concept of what a sacrifice is.

The sacrificial system is a central part of the early Old Testament. The concept is often described in the three primary books of the Law—Leviticus, Numbers, and Deuteronomy. It is focused particularly well for our context in Leviticus 16 in connection with the "sin offering." The people of Israel were on the Exodus searching for the Promised Land. For these nomadic people, while sacrifices had many purposes, they all stemmed from one basic need. They needed some tangible way to express their repentance to God for their sin and to receive, and be aware that they were receiving, God's forgiveness. The offering of a sacrifice provided an ideal vehicle to meet that need. The very best animal in the flock, a lamb or a bull, was selected to be given to God in sacrifice. Nothing but the finest would do. A goat was also selected but was not to be slain. On a chosen day (the Day of Atonement being the most sacred of such days each year) the people of Israel were called to gather in front of the tent of meeting (the forerunner of the Temple). A Levite was chosen to enter the tent of meeting to kill the sacrificial animal on the altar. A portion of the blood of the animal was then sprinkled on the altar as an offering of repentance to God. Some time later another portion of the blood was carried outside the tent and sprinkled on the live goat in the presence of the people. The goat was then chased into the wilderness, never to return, the blood on its head symbolizing the sins of the people being carried away and thus forgiven by God. The principle underlying the sacrifice was that, the best having been given, the remainder was sanctified, forgiven and made whole by God's generosity. The remainder, of course, was not the remainder of the animal flock, but God's flock, his chosen people. The effect of the sacrifice was not to lose something in the giving but to give the best of something so that what remained could be changed, renewed, and made clean. That is the essence of making a sacrifice, as the Old Testament describes it.

The principle of giving the best of something in order that what remains can be made stronger and more adequate is not confined to the Old Testament nor exclusively to the forgiveness of sin.

For example, (if I may paraphrase the action freely) God has said to us, "I want to be a part of your life and to add quality to the days of your life. To allow me to do that most effectively, I am asking you to give a part of your time, the best part of your time, exclusively and entirely to me. I am asking you to make a sacrifice." So God said to his people, "Remember the sabbath day, to keep it holy," the fourth commandment. The idea of the commandment, if one can presume to know God's thoughts, was not to separate one day out of the week for God, but to observe one day each week especially with God so that God could better and more effectively bless and hallow the remaining days of the week as well.

Or, to bring the sacrificial principle into our individual daily experience more directly, those who maintain a daily prayer discipline will understand this best. If we set aside a time to pray each day, those minutes we give to God have a way of changing the complexion and the quality of the whole day. In giving God a part of the day as a sacrifice, through that action we are inviting him to enter more effectively the entire day and give it greater substance and quality. Indeed, I sense the reality of that most clearly when, for some reason, I fail to give God that prayer time in the morning. When I neglect that time too often or too many days in a row, somehow the days are different for me and not in a positive way. That is the sacrificial giving of time. Give God a portion of the day exclusively, as in prayer, Bible reading and/or meditation, and God will hallow, bless, and change the whole of your day.

Or, to take that principle into a broader area of our lives, God has said to us, "I want to put quality and substance into all of your relationships. To allow me to do that most effectively, I am asking you to accept and live by a special set of expectations in one relationship. The marriage relationship, unlike any other, is to be life-long and exclusive. Offer me that faithfully in your life, make me that sacrifice, and I will add quality to all your relationships. Gladly and faithfully accepting a special and exclusive set of expectations in a primary relationship opens the door for God to bless and hallow other relationships as well. Now, don't put the book down and go tell your spouse that your marriage relationship is a sacrifice without explaining exactly what you mean! But do look around you and see how often it is that the people who have solid, quality marriage relationships are the very same people whose relationships beyond their marriages—with their children, their neighbors and friends, even with you—are also characterized by quality.

Further illustrations of the principle abound, and the reader can easily discover his or her own. *The sacrificial principle* is that we offer a portion, the best portion, to God. God in turn has a way of blessing and redeeming the remainder to make it more adequate and holy. This is not a bargain we make with God. It is an accurate observation over the centuries about how God works with us.

The conversion of that principle into the idea of sacrificial giving is easy, yet it represents a dramatic shift from what we often think. *To give to God sacrificially is to give a portion of our money, the best portion, in order that God may bless and hallow the remainder and make it more adequate.* Giving a portion means giving a responsibly calculated portion. Giving the best portion means giving it first, off the top of our income before other things are cared for. Making the remainder more adequate means just what it says. God's promise is that giving sacrificially means that what remains will be more than adequate to meet our needs. Further, our money and our attitude toward it will be redeemed, and the power it has to dominate us will be broken.

Did Jesus not say, "Give, and it will be given to you; good measure, pressed down, shaken together, running over, will be put into your lap. For the measure you give will be the measure you get back"? Sometimes reading those direct words we are so tempted to spiritualize them to make them mean everything that they end up meaning nothing. Indeed, that is one way to take both the force and clarity out of Jesus' direct instruction "to give" and out of the promise he makes, "that it will be given to you." To be sure, the words refer to far more than the giving of money. But is it not possible that the words are a New Testament statement of the sacrificial principle and that they mean exactly what they say? Is it not possible that one thing they do in fact mean is that when we give sacrificially of our financial resources, in proportion to our income, it is God's promise that we will receive in full measure, pressed down and running over, everything essential that we need for our life? In order to experience that, as thousands have experienced it, we must first offer our sacrifice, first become responsible givers. But in the sacrifice we open channels for God to bless the remainder effectively, indeed, to give us what we need in abundance.

I have in fact experienced that very thing, not as a possibility but as a reality in my own life. My wife and I have been sacrificial givers for many years and long before we could have defined it in this sense. We both grew up in families where giving was a normal part of our church life. From childhood on, we put our pennies in the offering every Sunday. We shared another experience as well. We were both brought up to believe that our gift was not to the Church as much as it was to God, and that it formed part of our relationship with God. When we married, giving was already something we held dear. We struggled with how to manage it and what to give. That struggle was accentuated in our early married life because God was a great deal more generous in giving us children than he was in giving us salary. In those early days, in fact, there were many months when the money ran out. Putting our offering, a pittance, in the envelope on the last Sunday of the month sometimes took all that was left. It was sometimes a matter of paying our pledge or buying the groceries that were needed. To be honest, the pledge did not always win, so we soon learned to fill all the envelopes for the month when we got paid so as not to have to face the temptation of neglecting the last Sunday's envelope when the check book couldn't stand it. Please understand that it never occurred to us that we were poor or somehow being deprived. We simply solved the moral dilemma of the pledge by "paying off the top," even before we knew what the phrase meant, and trusting that all would work out by month's end.

We were also very lucky. That's how we understood it then. With amazing consistency, at the end of those months when the money would not stretch, something would happen. Occasionally a baptism for an unchurched family passing through town had to be done. Sometimes a small wedding had to be performed on short notice (for which there were many reasons).

In each case there was a small gift given. Far more often a funeral had to be conducted. The funeral director in this northern Minnesota town was a parish member. So I was called fairly frequently to conduct simple burial services for indigent lumberjacks and the unchurched people in the area. The five dollar fee for such services was often the difference that made our money stretch the extra day or two until the next pay day. I say we thought we were lucky. It was only much later that we came to understand that something else was happening—that as we tried to be faithful to God in our giving, he too was being faithful to us in seeing that what remained was enough to meet our needs.

The first dim light of God's part in this came when our first child was born. We had no hospitalization insurance, so we tried to save enough to cover the hospital bill. My wife remembers it to have been about $200 in 1955. We also saved for the doctor, but we knew we wouldn't have enough for both. Our feeling was that our baby would not really be ours until the bills were paid. When the hospital bill was paid we had about $60 left. The doctor's fees according to his printed schedule were to be $90. When the bill arrived the doctor had reduced the bill by one third in what he called a "professional courtesy." It was for $60. This was a total surprise to us. I must confess that at the time our rejoicing was confined to knowing that we had our son free and clear. But we were also beginning to get an inkling that something else was involved here.

It came in better perspective when, many years later in a Bible study we taught, we came to Paul's words in II Corinthians. In the context of asking the Corinthians to be "cheerful givers," Paul wrote, "And God is able to provide you with every blessing in abundance, so that you may always have enough . . ." (II Corinthians 9:8). Then the timely funerals and the professional courtesy were remembered, and we began to allow ourselves to think that they were more than simple coincidence.

Over the years that followed, God continued to bless us generously with children, but not so generously with salary. We continued to give in proportion to our income and to try to teach others to do so as well. We also continued to "pay it off the top" by filling all the month's envelopes at the first of the month. In fact, every time we failed to do that our church pledge fell behind and was a burden to pay. While we were not entirely aware of it, our dependence on God to provide deepened and deepened. We never had a lot and we worried over the bills virtually every month, but one way or another we always seemed to have enough.

Then it was time for college. In preparation for that my wife went to work to begin a college fund for our five children. Since she was trained as an elementary school teacher/librarian and since a good job was available, it seemed like a good idea. But I am helpless in a household. Our children needed a mother at home and I needed a wife at home. So, after a year she gave up her job. We said to one another, "If God wants these kids to go to college, he will have to find another way." And he did!

A group in our parish came to us, asking if we would allow them to start a college fund that would provide $1,000 a year per child while our children were undergraduates. That was a "God-send" in the truest sense of the word. With scholarships and grants, for which we scoured the catalogues, and what our children could earn and save, together with what we could afford, this gift provided just enough for each one each year. With three children in college or graduate school in each of six consecutive years, that gift made the difference.

After six years, however, we decided that we had accepted enough. We thanked the people who had helped so tremendously, and with one child beginning her junior year and another still in high school, we struck out on our own. We did not know when we began whence the $1,000 for our college daughter would come. That summer three friends wrote us letters, each one, incidentally, including a $100 bill to help our daughter with college. In August we were notified that her college grant would be $500 higher than it had ever been for any of our other children. It was so unusual that we made several phone calls to check on it before we would believe it. That totaled $800 we had not expected. While the first gifts aroused gratitude, this new $500 povoked us to say, "All right, Lord, that's 80 percent of it. How are you going to provide the remaining $200?" In the first week of school our daughter was offered a job in the school library, a job that opened up because another student had decided at the last minute not to take it. That job provided not $200, but $200 a month for nine months. On the day we were called and told about that, my wife and I independently came to see and talk about the same thing. Jesus said, "Give, and it will be given to you; good measure, pressed down, shaken together, running over, will be put into your lap."

The significance of those words weighed heavily on us because in our summer's search for the $1,000, while we couldn't seriously consider cutting our church pledge, we did seriously consider postponing payment on a special Venture in Mission pledge if we had to find part of the money. We decided not to do that. It was in that context that Jesus' words, "Give and it shall be given to you . . . ," could no longer remain an isolated principle called "sacrificial giving" but became a fact of life from our gracious God.

. It almost seems superfluous to say that the next spring, as our daughter looked toward her senior year, a grant of $1,000 came from a source of which we had never dreamed, which supplied the need for the final year.

I write all this, not principally to tell about our experience, although I believe that has value, but because our experience can be multiplied hundreds of thousands of times in the lives of other faithful Christian people. God can be trusted if we are willing to risk with him.

I do not want to be misunderstood in any of this. I have pinpointed financial matters because that is our context. God's generosity to us has not always been financial. More often than not it is not financial. Our attempt over the years to be faithful stewards has been a vehicle to help us understand that God really cares about us; that he expects us to let him in as a full partner in all areas of our life; and that, when we are willing to risk enough to do that, he is truly dependable, truly faithful.

The Hebrews of the Old Testament perhaps understood that better than we do. With God's guidance they saw that when they offered the best they had, the finest portion of the whole to God, God in turn was enabled to bless, hallow, strengthen, and make more adequate what remained. Their experience in the primitive offering of sacrifices was that God could be trusted. Our experience through sacrificial giving is, and can be, the same.

Chapter 4

To Tithe or Not to Tithe — An Ancient Standard Rediscovered

In 1982 at its General Convention in New Orleans, the Episcopal Church affirmed the tithe as the "minimum standard of giving for Christians." While we are a long way from being a leader in this matter among the various Christian bodies, for Episcoplians this was a historic action, since every previous effort to proclaim officially any standard of financial stewardship had been watered down into meaninglessness or defeated.

In the first edition of this book, published in 1975, a negative position in regard to tithing was taken. Tithing was felt then to be (1) legalistic, (2) an Old Testament concept not stressed in the New Testament, (3) a "dream concept" without a base of wide acceptance, and (4) judgmental on those who chose not to or could not meet its demands.

Since I was privileged to be among the leaders proposing the tithing resolution in New Orleans, obviously much has happened in mind and in my experience since 1975. Like the Church of which I am a member and a priest, I have revised my position completely. In this reversal I take comfort in the words of an anonymous editorialist who wrote, "No one ought ever to be afraid to change his mind, since it only means that he is smarter today than he was yesterday."

It is beyond question that the tithe is the standard of financial stewardship set out in the Old Testament. In seven Old Testament books (Leviticus, Numbers, Deuteronomy, I Samuel, II Chronicles, Amos and Malachi) "tithing" or "giving the tenth part" is mentioned forty-nine times in thirty-seven separate incidents. In several such references it is stated as "the law." In several other references the failure to tithe is presented as a symptom of unfaithfulness of the people of Israel. It is in that vein that the prophet Malachi writes in 3:7–10,

> From the days of your fathers you have turned aside from my statutes and have not kept them. Return to me, and I will return to you, says the Lord of hosts. But you say, "How shall we return?" Will a man rob God? Yet you are robbing me. But you say, "How are we robbing thee?" In your tithes and offerings. . . . You are robbing me; the whole nation of you. Bring the full tithes into the storehouse, that there may be food in the house; and thereby put me to the test, says the Lord of hosts, if I will not open the windows of heaven for you and pour down for you an overflowing blessing.

The New Testament has but four references to tithing. One is in Hebrews 7:4–9 and is used only to describe a function of the Levitical priesthood. The other three are in the Gospels of Matthew and Luke. One of these is in the parable of the Pharisee and the publicam (Luke 18:12). The other two appear to be parallel passages of a single event in which Jesus is fiercely critical of the Pharisees (Matthew 23:23 and Luke 11:42).

Having done the foregoing cursory analysis, for many years I was impressed by the meager references to tithing in the New Testament. I interpreted the lack of references to mean that tithing was no longer an issue of consequence for Christians. I further reasoned that the New Testament standard of giving was not 10 percent but 100 percent. What God asked of a Christian disciple was 100 percent, given in a life lived in obedience to Jesus Christ as his Savior and Lord, a life lived "in Christ," to use Paul's phrase. Since I could not easily give 100 percent of either my life or my money, nor did I find anyone except Christ expecting me to, I was then free to give whatever I chose to give of both. I usually chose to give something less than 100 percent of my life to God and substantially less than 10 percent of my money.

For reasons of which I am not now fully aware, sometime ago I was led to go back to those New Testament references for a closer look. What I discovered was that tithing is seldom mentioned in the New Testament because, in Jesus' mind, it was simply assumed as normal and expected. It was so obvious a standard that it was beyond the need of discussion.

Note how Jesus deals with it as both Matthew and Luke report it. In Matthew 23:23 Jesus harshly criticizes the Pharisees for tithing "mint and dill and cummin," and neglecting "the weightier matters of the law, justice and mercy and faith. . . ." Now note carefully what Jesus says next. *"These you ought to have done."* He is critical of them because they made no connection between their tithing and their ethical behavior. They tithed but did not go to the weightier matters, translating the faith that brought them to tithe into the faith that produced and championed justice, mercy and faith. In effect what Jesus says is this: Tithe? Of course we tithe! We don't need to discuss it. Just do it! But having done it, don't think you have done it all. Tithing is only the beginning. Do it! Now, let's get on to the weightier stuff—living your life in justice, mercy, and faith. Luke's Gospel presents Jesus' words in much the same way. Having judged the Pharisees for tithing but neglecting "justice and the love of God," Luke also records Jesus' further explanatory words, *"these you ought to have done,"* that is, you ought to have tithed, "without neglecting the others" (Luke 11:42).

From the perspective of both the Old and New Testaments and the words of Jesus a strong case is made for tithing as the biblical norm of our financial stewardship.

Further, while tithing may have many legitimate meanings in our time, in the Scripture it has only one meaning, the meaning from which the word itself is derived. The tithe is a measure of one-tenth of the whole.

It can be argued that tithing, that is, dedicating 10 percent of our income back to God, does not necessarily mean it must go to the Church. Both in the times of the Old and New Testaments, the major and often only source of support for social services and education was the religious establishment. In our time many of those functions have been taken over by the government or private agencies. It is appropriate, therefore, if we choose to split the tithe between the Church and other charities. But having said that because I believe it to be true, I must also admit to a little hesitation about such a split born out of personal experience. For some years my wife and I believed and thought we were following the so-called modern tithe. Five percent of our gross income was dedicated to God through the Church and another 5 percent was dedicated through other charities. What we discovered over several years, however, was that the Church's 5 percent was always paid. However, we would have had to tell the proverbial "fish story" to stretch our other charitable gifts to make an additional 5 percent. The fact was that the first was faithfully taken care of while the second rather haphazardly chosen charitable gifts seldom ran much over an additional 2 percent. When we discovered how we were hiding behind what sounded like a reasonable system, we shifted and pledged ourselves to give 8 percent to God through the Church and 2 percent elsewhere. We also committed almost all of that 2 percent to specific programs early in the year to be sure that it, in fact, was used as we wanted it to be used. There are many who, like good friends of ours, set up a special tithe account and put 10 percent of their earnings into it each pay period. That account is untouchable except for giving. They derive immense joy and satisfaction as faithful disciples and stewards from using it to pay their church pledge weekly and deciding periodically where to give the remainder.

It has also been said that the tithe is discriminatory, laying a heavier burden on the poor than on the rich. From the standpoint of having available discretionary income, clearly the middle income and more affluent groups have more money available from which to give. Having grown up and lived the first ten years of my married life in an income bracket that would now be labeled as below the poverty line, I believe such a claim deserves a more careful analysis than that. In fact, it needs a more careful analysis than our space permits. However, some elements essential to such an analysis might be indicated by these few comments.

The purpose of the tithe in the Scripture is not to raise money for the Church. Indeed, any tithing program in our day that has nothing but money-raising as its fundamental purpose, while it may succeed for a time, will eventually fail. As is stressed in this book, we give as a fundamental part of our relationship with God. If Scripture is to be believed, one of the things God has promised in that relationship is that, when we are faithful stewards, that which remains to us will be made adequate to meet our needs. *"Give, and it will be given to you; full measure pressed down, shaken together, will be put into your lap"* (Luke 6:38). Or, again to use the words of the prophet Malachi, who speaks for God, "Bring the full tithes into the storehouse . . . *and thereby put me to the test*, says the Lord of hosts, *if I will not open the windows of heaven for you and pour down for you an overflowing blessing.*" (Malachi 3:10).

St. Paul says the same in II Corinthians 9:6–10. "The point is this: he who sows sparingly will also reap sparingly, and he who sows bountifully will reap bountifully. . . . God loves a cheerful giver. And God is able to *provide you with every blessing in abundance, so that you may always have enough of everything. . . .* He who supplies seed to the sower and bread for food will supply and multiply your resources . . . ."

The implication in these passages is that it is partly through our faithful giving that God is enabled to use the remainder to make it adequate to meet our needs.

If what we are about in stewardship is simply raising money, the poor should be exempt. If what we are about, however, is putting people into closer touch with God and with God's blessings through our giving, as the Scripture promises, no one should be prevented by any circumstance from being a part of that.

In fact, the poor seem to know that better than some of their advocates. In statistics developed among its own members by the Episcopal Church nationally, in the area of stewardship two groups stood out as the largest in their approval of and participation in tithing. They were (1) the lowest income group and (2) those who were single parents, generally a low income group.

Sometime ago I led a stewardship conference for a southwestern diocese. In one of the discussion periods a canvasser told of calling on an elderly widow for a pledge. Seeing the woman in what the caller called "her poverty circumstances," he just couldn't bring himself to ask for the pledge. When the woman volunteered a small pledge he did not encourage it and only accepted it at the woman's insistence. His reasoning was that she could not afford to live adequately, much less give anything away. I was moved to say to him, as gently as I knew how, that he almost took away from that woman one of the few things she had left to give. She could no longer come to church. She could no longer give her time or talent, but she could give this. I don't know if the gift was a tithe or anywhere near it. But that's not the point. The point is to question why we insist on putting such people into a category labelled "poor" and then take away from them one of the few things they have left that can give them a sense of offering to God and a tangible part in the ministry of the Body of Christ.

Having said this, I must say also that the attitude with which we give is as important for our spiritual well-being as the standard or system we use to calculate our giving. St. Paul said it best when he wrote in words already quoted in this chapter, "God loves a cheerful giver." Some years ago there was a motto going around that played on these words. It read, "God loves a cheerful giver but he'll take money from a grouch." I suppose that's cute, but it cynically misses the point. The attitude with which we return to God of his blessings to us is at the heart of our relationship with God. If our stewardship is fundamentally a statement we make about the quality of that relationship, as we have argued in this book that it is, then a stated percentage gift only partially expresses our stewardship before God. It is not enough for us to be responsible to God in our giving. It is not enough to relate ourselves principally to God as a steward to a master. It is only enough when we go on into the deeper and more fundamental relationship the New Testament offers, that of a son or daughter to a father. We are called to give joyfully as well as responsibly because God is not so much someone who entrusts his property to a steward as he is one who gives his love to his children.

Try, for example, to let the words "steward" and "child" roll around in your imagination. To be a faithful steward in your relationship with God is to give priority in your Christian life to such qualities as faithfulness, responsibility and integrity. But state your relationship with God just slightly differently and see the enormous change in attitude that it provokes. You are God's child and are called to exercise your responsibilities as a son or daughter. Here the qualities of that relationship are thankfulness, love, joy, companionship and intimacy. To be sure, both sets of qualities, those of the steward and those of the child, are part of our Christian response to God. But it is the latter that are primary. It is in the latter alone that we can be "cheerful givers." It is in the latter alone that we can see that it is not a portion of what we have that belongs to God and must therefore be returned. All that we have is God's, is the Father's, and far from returning that portion which is God's because it is due from a faithful steward, we are called to return all of what we are given because we are part of the family; we are loved as children. We return all of it, some in service, some in prayer, some in the quality of our relationships, some in talent developed and used, some in a life consecrated to God, and some in specific material gifts, gifts of money thankfully calculated out of that part of his bounty to us. It is as sons and daughters that we are motivated to give cheerfully and thankfully. It is as stewards that we are led to be responsible about our giving.

The Rt. Rev. Basil Guy, Bishop of Bedford, Church of England, writing in a booklet titled *Stewardship Facts*, published by the National Council of Churches, describes stewardship in this way:

> It is, of course, most happily true that whenever we begin to tackle seriously any one part of the Christian life, all the rest of life begins to come into sharper focus. It has been—and we thank God for it—the experience of many places that a stewardship campaign quickens and deepens the whole of church life in a parish. But that does not alter the fact that stewardship is not a gospel, but a discipline. . . .

Sometime and somehow every conscientious Christian must translate all the rhetoric and commitment into a number on a pledge card. Is there a discipline that can help in translation?

We have already commended tithing, which we understand to mean 10 percent of all income. I am often asked, "Does that mean before or after taxes?" My answer is always the same. "I don't care. That's between you and God."

I am also often asked how a family or person can move toward tithing if they have never done it before, and a jump to the tithe is too big a step to take all at once. The answer is a system called proportionate giving. It can be described very easily. Take your annual gross income and simply multiply it by the percentage (3, 5, 6 percent) with which you want to begin, the percentage that you believe is the responsible portion for you. Then, in the case of an annual gift to God through the Church, simply divide that amount by the frequency with which the gift will be made in one year (fifty-two if weekly, four if quarterly, etc.).

For most church people who are already making a gift, it might be more useful to begin where you are. Take your annual gross income and divide it into your present annual giving out of that income. This will give you the percentage of your income that the gift really represents. Then determine what proportion of your income you would like to share, to return materially to God. Multiply your gross income by that percentage, and so on. As you can see this can, and should, be put in very specific terms in relation to a church pledge.

For example: If your annual gross income is $10,000 a year and you give $2 a week to God through your church, then it is helpful to know that your gift represents 1 percent of your income.

Or, if your annual gross income is $15,000 a year and you give $5 a week to God through your church, your gift represents 1.7 percent of your income.

If your annual gross income is $25,000 a year and you give $500 a year to God through your church, your gift represents 2 percent of your income.

Often churches develop a chart that helps their members with the mathematics. The figures that would be most helpful to use would, of course, be those that most closely match the incomes of the people in your congregation. In your presentation of proportionate giving you might want to produce a chart like the one below, with the income figures again matching those of your members.

A Guide to Proportionate Giving

Your proportionate weekly gift would be:

If your annual gross income is:	3%	4%	5%	10%	12%
$ 8,000	$4.62	$6.15	$7.70	$15.40	$18.46
9,000					
10,000					
12,000					
15,000					
17,500					
20,000					
25,000					
50,000	26.92	38.46	48.00	96.00	115.38

Note some elements in constructing such a chart. (1) The matter is stated positively. It does not say "if you wish to become a proportionate giver." It assumes that what has been said, verbally and in print, about proportionate giving has been heard and will be acted upon. (2) The chart also begins at 3 percent as the lowest figure. Seventy-five to ninety percent of your congregation are probably now giving below that amount. The chart sets their sights a little higher at the start to show them what is really possible for them. (3) It also doesn't stop at 10 percent as though that were the optimum gift. It shatters any limits, low or high, thus speaking to the principle of this way of giving without fetters. (4) The chart speaks of gifts as weekly amounts. While monthly, quarterly, and annual giving are perfectly acceptable, for most people weekly giving allows greater freedom to consider a more substantial return to God without the emotional impact of the larger annual amount to temper a responsible and generous impulse. This is not to manipulate people into giving more than they can afford. But it is to give them the freedom to stretch their responding muscles to see further into what is really within their reach, what is really possible for them. More than that, a weekly gift has an appropriateness that matches the concurrent weekly offering of worship in which they engage. However, since income is earned and paid in varying ways, some flexibility needs to remain in any system like this. (5) The amounts represented by the proportionate gifts will seldom come out to an even dollar amount. That has the real value of moving away from the prison that puts gifts in round numbers without basing the giving on any systematic measure. It underlines the focus on the percentage, the proportion that is given. A weekly gift of an odd amount, like $9.23 for example, will be a continual reminder of the principle and will be a constant affirmation of the person as a proportionate giver every time the check is written all year long.

However the principle of proportionate giving is presented, the major advantages remain the same.

1. It puts the emphasis on giving out of income, where it belongs.

2. It allows the giver to consider and compute his or her gift according to a solid principle, giving him or her the freedom to determine how that principle will be applied in his or her personal response on a pledge card.

3. It keeps persons honest about their giving, honest about the real value of their gift in relation to what they have. The measure is not, as it tends to be by pure dollar amounts, against what others with more can give (imagined negative affirmation) or against what others with less are able to give (imagined positive affirmation). The measure remains where it needs to be—yourself against yourself—what you give against what you have.

4. It allows every person who participates to stand on equal ground as a giver. The giver with modest income who gives 5 percent of that income is able to be affirmed in his or her giving along with the big giver who gives 5 percent of a much larger income. Their dollar amounts will vary considerably, but each is sharing equally with God through the Church out of what that person has.

5. Most significantly, it provides for those who want to be conscientious in their stewardship response to God, a way to respond responsibly and thankfully and to know that their response has been carefully considered to the best of their ability.

Perhaps a final word is in order in regard to the power of proportionate giving. It seems to me that power flows in two directions, to the giver and to the receiver. We have alluded before to the need of people to know and to feel that they are okay—okay with their fellows and okay with God. Clearly, participating in proportionate giving will not provide the total affirmation that they need from other persons or God. But it is deeply affirming to all people to know that they have seriously and conscientiously faced a daily issue in their lives—the issue of the way they will use their money—seen a positive way of responding to it, and made the appropriate response. Call it affirmation or satisfaction or fulfillment or whatever. It is there.

In 1973, the *Lutheran Standard* did a survey of some church members who had been proportionate givers in the previous few years. Some of the results were printed in a bimonthly newsletter titled *S.A.L.T.* Here is a sample of comments that were made, indicating the power of proportionate giving.

I first felt good about giving about three years ago. The turning point, I think, was when I realized that Christ really loved me. I understood that all we have is from God, that we should return a portion of that to Him. But those things never really made it with me. I relate better to things Christ had to teach us, the things about loving. As Paul said, ". . . the greatest of these is love." I feel now when I give, I'm about his business of loving and it's great. [An electrical engineer]

The difference is feeling good about giving instead of feeling obligated. My giving to other things (family, friends, other charities) has increased considerably. [A university extension dairy agent]

We have learned that there is joy and satisfaction in giving proportionately . . . we have never been in need of anything, and every decision on our part to give more has invariably resulted in more (and unexpected) blessing, both monetary and otherwise. Putting the Lord first with your pocketbook helps you in putting the Lord first in other areas of your life. [An owner of a construction company]

They say miracles don't happen today, but we have had them happen in our lives since we pledged proportionate giving. Logically, we cannot explain how there were dollars to pay bills after writing our check to the church; how, at just the right time, job security came our way. As far as we are concerned you cannot afford not to be a proportionate giver. [An optician]

The experience mainly was deeper faith, love, and relationship to the Lord. It is just a joy I cannot explain. [A milkman]

(*S.A.L.T.*, vol. 4, March–April 1973)

These families were identified as living in five widely scattered states from coast to coast, as having annual incomes ranging from $10,000 to $25,000, and as giving from 6 to 11 percent of income to church and charities combined. And one cannot help but observe how little their comments connected their giving to parish loyalty or program, in which they were deeply involved, and how central to their feelings were things like faith, joy, loving, and their sense of the Lord in their lives. These are not isolated individuals carefully selected, but are representative of the experience of thousands who have seen the power of proportionate giving to affirm them as persons and to work in their own lives.

Quite clearly, the other direction in which the power of proportionate giving flows is toward the receiver of these gifts; in our context, the parish church. To receive even minimum proportionate pledges from all of its member families would be a financial boon beyond imagining in most parishes. Indeed, it puts financial worries to rest in those places where it is significantly practiced by the members.

Recently, I saw the results of a study done in the Episcopal Church. It was calculated that if every Episcopal family in the nation were suddenly to become destitute and all of us were to go on Social Security at the lowest family income level, and then, if all of us, at that income level, were to give a proportionate gift of 5 percent to God through the Church, the income of the Church for God's work would increase by seven times over. That's the power of proportionate giving to multiply parish income!

But more than the obvious financial results of such giving, there is another equally powerful consequence. In situations where proportionate giving has really taken hold, and where normal parish financial problems have been virtually eliminated, people seldom hold an attitude of complacency in their parish prosperity. Indeed, the feeling in such places is rather one of urgency—urgency about ministry both at home and away. One might guess that the urgency surfaced in the vacuum created where discussions of parish money problems had once been. But I think not. The more likely possibility is that the urgency came from the givers who extended their own stewardship into the life of the parish and led the parish as a whole to become a more responsible steward in ministry. Whatever the explanation, there are few of us who would not delight in that kind of urgency as a replacement to the urgency we all too often feel to meet the budget and see that all the bills get paid. Such is the promise and the power of proportionate giving as a way to express our thanksgiving to God.

This matter might well be summed up by an incident reported to be the true experience of an employee of the Internal Revenue Service.

The other day I checked a queer return. Some guy with an income of $5,000 claimed he gave $624 to some church. Sure, he was within the 20 percent limit, but it looked a little suspicious to me. So I dropped in on the guy and asked about his return. "Have you a receipt from the church?" I asked, figuring that would make him squirm. "Sure," he said, and off he went to bring the receipts. Well, he had me. One look and I knew he was on the level. So I apologized for bothering him, explaining I had to check out deductions that seemed unusually high. Upon leaving, he invited me to attend church with him. "Thanks, but I belong to a church myself," I replied. As I rode home, I couldn't help thinking about the man's interest in and fondness for his church and his unembarrassed, open invitation to me. I wondered, a little enviously, where he got his enthusiasm. It wasn't until Sunday morning when I put my usual two dollars in the offering plate that it came to me.

Chapter 5

Learning From the Grassroots

For three years, from 1979 to 1982, I served as Chairman of the General Convention Standing Commission on Stewardship, a national level committee of the Episcopal Church. It was a newly created body reflecting the increasing awareness of the importance of stewardship in the life of the church.

In the course of our meetings we spent a great deal of time exploring and working over the problem areas we saw. While this was essential and helpful, it occurred to me after one especially hard session how typical it was for us, in many areas of concern, to spend the bulk of our time addressing the problems and only a little of our time looking at places and people where effective solutions are being implemented. I began to wonder where the effective stewardship programs were being carried out at the level of the local congregation and if there were any common elements in them that could teach us something. The commission authorized me, on their behalf, to pursue this line of thought.

The effort involved contacting all the diocesan bishops of the Episcopal Church to ask them to identify three to five parish congregations in their diocese which, in the bishop's observation and opinion, were doing the best work in stewardship. No effort was made to define what "the best" meant. That was left to each bishop's discretion. Close to 60 percent of the bishops responded to my letter, identifying some 264 parishes nationwide. A letter was then sent to each of these congregations asking them to respond, in three typewritten pages or less, to three very general questions.

1. Of what does your stewardship program consist?
2. How do you execute that program?
3. How do you feel about what you are doing?

Seventy-four parishes, or 28 percent, responded within the time frame with which I had to work. I had expected certain similarities to appear in the responses. I had no idea that the similarities would be so pronounced.

The following are the highlights of those responses together with some excerpts from a few individual returns. It must be said that by the standards of professional pollsters neither the sample nor the methods of gathering this data would be considered scientific. It was not my intention to be professionally scientific but simply to hear directly from some of those who, in someone's educated opinion, were doing an effective job in stewardship. The results are at least interesting, and at best suggest some avenues of serious thought. (These findings are printed here with the permission of the Standing Commission.)

GRASS ROOTS SURVEY RESULTS — 1980–81
Data Gathered and Analyzed
by
The Rev. John H. MacNaughton
for the
General Convention Standing Commission
on Stewardship/Development
Findings Based on 74 Replies from 264 Parishes Identified
by a Diocesan Bishop as Being Strong in Stewardship

1. *Many clergy were surprised to have been identified by their bishop as strong in this area.* Undoubtedly this means that we have various definitions of what an "effective job" is. It also suggests that those doing an effective job continue to struggle to become even more effective, the strugglers being less easily satisfied with their progress than an outside observer, such as the bishop. It further suggests that the best stewardship is done when it is seen as a normal part of the

ongoing, year-round life of a parish. When it is a natural part of parish life, we are less aware of the impact it has on an observer.

2. *The theology of stewardship is strikingly similar.* The almost universal base of stewardship in effective parishes is the base of thanksgiving for God's gifts. God is the owner of all our resources. We are the users, the stewards of all things during our lifetime. The text, "All things come of thee, O Lord, and of thine own have we given thee," is experientially seen to be the truth that must be taught and acted upon.

3. *A significant number of the responses went a step further and identified stewardship as a discipline.* How we as stewards deal with God's gifts, how we actually think about and use our gifts of time, talent and treasure, is the most accurate measure of the depth and quality of our spiritual life. Some indicated that making this connection was at the heart of our understanding and the basis of our response in stewardship. The separation of the sacred and the secular in human life was denied as representing reality. The truth is that how we think about and use what we tend to call the secular, that is, our material possessions, is a direct reflection of what we are and believe as persons. It is a measure of our spiritual depth and awareness.

4. *Overwhelmingly, the tithe was identified as the standard, or minimum standard, of Christian giving.* While there are many definitions of "tithing" current in the Church, the responses generally identified the tithe as 10 percent of our gross income from all sources, without further qualification. It was also identified as the biblical standard of both the Old and New Testaments. Further, proportionate giving, i.e., returning to God a proportion, a percentage of our income, was identified as the working principle with which responsible stewardship begins. Working up to a 10 percent tithe and beyond was identified as the goal of responsible stewardship. The quality of the comments received on this issue

was strong; the tithe was treated not as an interesting but impossible standard but as a norm from which many respondents were unwilling to move.

5. *There were very few (only three of seventy-four) steward-ship programs based on a preset parish budget.* Among those identified as effective in stewardship, raising money to meet a pre-prepared budget has virtually disappeared.

6. *A great many emphasized the presentation of parish goals, particularly in relation to work outside the parish, in the diocese or the world, and/or new work within the parish as a stimulus to a stewardship response.* There was almost no mention of budget increases caused by inflation, etc., but the presentation of new thrusts, new work, new or increased outreach was the key in these responses.

7. *Almost without exception, the clergy were identified as actively involved in stewardship teaching and program-ming.* The role of the clergy was seen in planning, writing, preaching and teaching, and setting up and working with organizational structures to do stewardship. Many worked with active committees of lay people but most took a strong leadership role themselves as well.

8. *The organization of parish people to do stewardship was reported in most responses as being tight and detailed.* There was a great variety of organization styles, but common to them all were built-in standards and expectations set down for every person and job in stewardship. Much was expected from people who worked in this area and thus, according to our responses, much was accomplished.

9. *Overwhelmingly, the respondents talked about steward-ship as a year-round process and not just involved with the Every Member Canvass.* Details on how stewardship was presented and acted out in parish life year-round were not as detailed, but conviction about the principles was strong and clear.

10. *Many outside resources were mentioned positively.* Among those mentioned most were:

A. The Alabama Plan or some adaptation of it.

B. A diocesan plan that had been developed in a particular diocese that was significantly supportive and helpful.

C. The book, *Stewardship: Myths and Methods*, was seen as helpful.

D. The improved material of the national Church on stewardship was noted as more effective and useful.

11. *Significantly, very few mentioned the stewardship of time and talent in connection with the fall stewardship emphasis.* These belong as essentials of a year-round program, many said. In the fall the thrust was to concentrate on the stewardship of our material resources without the contamination of these other concerns at that time.

12. *The following comments appeared in some form in from five to fifteen of the responses,* not enough to be listed above, but enough to merit inclusion in our findings.

A. The effectiveness of stewardship teaching was seen in direct proportion to the effectiveness of the parish's ministry. The ministry of the parish was seen as a stewardship of its own. Where that stewardship of time, talent, treasure and concern, outreach and mission, was seen as having integrity and effectiveness, the stewardship response of the individual parish member was correspondingly deeper.

B. Stewardship teaching is a year-round need. However, regarding the stewardship of money, one appeal was made in the fall, inviting response. No special appeals were undertaken during the year that would tend to draw focus away from the fall program for pledges. Special needs that came up during the year were met by prior budget provisions, deliberately made following the fall canvass at budget time. Exceptions to this that were noted were Theological Education Sunday and the United Thank Offering.

C. Effective stewardship teaching required taking a risk, especially if the former way (here usually identified as raising money to meet a budget) had been moderately successful financially. To move away from that is to risk failure, but the potential rewards, spiritual as well as financial, were seen to be great.

D. Clergy need to lead in stewardship by example, even to the point of witnessing to their own pledge. The point made here by several respondents was that people need to know that the "theory of stewardship" we preach is matched by our practice. Several also said that lay people need to do the witnessing both for the value of the witness itself and so that the clergy are not "out there" all alone.

E. Part of the risk of entering into sound stewardship in a parish is that not everyone will get the message. Thus, several commented that we need to decide to work with and for those who will respond rather than retire with those who will not. Those who respond positively will increase in number and depth each year as stewardship as a spiritual discipline continues to be taught.

F. Some related their effective stewardship to various renewal experiences in the parish, i.e., Faith Alive, Cursillo, a charismatic experience, or some other parish or personal renewal experience.

G. A frequently reported method of coming to grips with and communicating a biblical and theological basis for stewardship was to ask the vestry to draft a statement of stewardship for the parish and then communicate this statement to the parish. This requires the vestry to wrestle with the basic biblical and theological issues and to lead the whole parish. In this connection, several reported that when vestries are challenged in this way they respond to the challenge positively and effectively.

H. Several commented on the need for honesty and parish involvement in the whole stewardship process. Everything needs to be up front, with nothing hidden from parish view. The idea to be communicated is that all are involved in it *together* as opposed to the feeling that some, i.e., the leadership, are doing it *to* the people.

I. As a parish asks, so it needs to live, using its financial resources and buildings in ministry to others outside the parish. This effort in outreach and ministry needs to be responsible both in its size and in the priority it has in total parish life. This also needs to be identified as the stewardship of the parish—a matter of integrity and consistency.

J. A significant number spoke of prayer as an integral part of their stewardship teaching. The stewardship effort is surrounded by the prayers of the leaders and people for God's guidance both in the individual's response and the parish response in using the resources that are generated.

A series of quotations from the responses we received follows, to give a flavor, to put clothes on the bare bones of this report.

Our thanks to the many who responded with such care and interest! We share this in the hope that you will see your response as having been a helpful use of your time and will find this information helpful yourself.

The Rev. R. Randolph Cooper
St. George's, 6904 West Avenue, San Antonio, TX 78213

Definition of Christian stewardship: "The systematic, proportionate, sacramental, and sacrificial giving of our time, talents and treasure, taking the tithe as our standard, to God through his Church on a weekly basis as a part of our worship, in obedience to his Word and in grateful thanksgiving for his redemptive love, with the firm conviction that everything that we have is a trust from God to be used in his service."

1. The priest's commitment to tithing: First and foremost the priest and rector of the parish must be fully committed to the principle of tithing. There can be no game playing with this. He must be willing to give as a pledge to the Church on a weekly basis 10% of all that he receives. That means 10% of

his salary, of his utilities, and of his housing and any other income that he might have. If he is furnished a house by the parish then he should figure his housing based on the form used by the national Church. If he is given a housing allowance then it is 10% of that. He then must be willing to witness to this pledge from the pulpit to his parish stating in dollar and cents amounts what he gives and why.

The Rev. Paul D. Edwards
Emmanuel, Fullerton, CA 92633

A second given is that the financial giving (stewardship) is a result of commitment to Jesus Christ as Lord and Savior. If one faces a financial problem one should not become involved in fund-raising enterprises but in commitment strategy. The former ends up in crash programs called that because the program itself usually crashes.

The most important stewardship decision we have made is to define the purpose of the Church. For us the purpose of the Church is to build Christian community, and the purpose of Christian community is to enable people to lead Christian lives. Nothing is done that does not support this purpose. Everyone of our groups must be working in this direction or cease to exist.

If it is true that financial giving is the fruit of commitment to Jesus Christ then we must concentrate on commitment to him; otherwise we are treating the symptom (poor giving) rather than the cause (poor commitment).

The Rev. Donald A. Seeks
St. Clement's, P. O. Box 505, Woodlake, CA 93286

The tithe (10%) is a biblical imperative for Christian giving. It is so ordered in the Old Testament (Gen. 14:20; Lev. 27:30; Num. 18:25,26). The full tithe has virtually the same importance as the various sacrifices (Deut. 12:10,11; Amos 4:4). Christ's death on the cross made animal sacrifices superfluous, but nothing superseded the command to tithe. Christian giving should begin with the tithe and continue with offerings beyond the tithe. To withhold either tithe or offerings is to rob God of his just due (Mal. 3:6–10). And to fulfill our proper stewardship is to see "the windows of heaven" open. It is God's promise that we will have "an overflowing blessing," which may or may not be material in nature. The Old Testament commands are confirmed by our Lord, albeit indirectly, when he upbraids the scribes and Pharisees for tithing all their household spices and yet "neglecting the weightier matters of the law," such as justice, mercy, and faith. Our Lord adds, *"These you ought to have done, without neglecting the others"* (Matt. 23:23; Luke 11:42).

The Rev. Edward E. Murphy
St. Luke's, 350 W. Yosemite Ave., Merced, CA 95340

Our philosophy is very simple:

1. If you are a serious Christian, you will tithe to the Church first (10% of income); after that you will decide what you will give.

2. While stewardship is far more than money, our money is the most critical part of it because we are materialistic, econocentric, and have a pocketbook-protection instinct greater than life preservation. I've preached many sermons on tithing and then giving after tithing.

The Rev. Cecil B. Jones, Jr.
All Saints, 608 Jefferson St., Tupelo, MS 38801

The basic premise of our stewardship theology is that all we are and all we have is a gift from God. God is the creator and owner of creation; we are his trusted managers (his stewards). As the owner of creation God gives us the freedom to use his creation as we choose. (That means we can act as if we are the owner if we choose to do so.) However, God is active in his creation and continually calls us to respond to him through our use of his gifts—we are a part of creation for the purpose of furthering his kingdom.

As we live in this world we are constantly provided opportunities of staying in touch with God. One of the primary ways we do this is through our actions as stewards. It is in our use of his creation that he speaks to us about our life-style and calls us to a deeper understanding of who we are and who he would have us be. The practice of stewardship is just that—practice. It requires a decision, a plan, and action.

One of the most effective ways to carry out the practice of stewardship is through proportionate giving. By committing myself to giving away a percentage of my income and time I am more able to stay in touch with God and his purpose. When we can begin to live our proportionate giving as a thankful response for all that has been given us, our relationship with God deepens and grows.

The Rev. Robert Sheeran
Grace Church, Kilmarnock, VA 22482

Our theology of stewardship is that stewardship is not a means of raising money, nor is it a way to support the church. It is not something that is emphasized at Every Member Canvass time only, but something that is preached and taught year-round and practiced by all the organizations within the parish—from the vestry down to the House of Young Churchmen. We teach that stewardship is composed of three elements:

1. Commitment, which is that which we believe about God and our Savior, Jesus Christ, and by which we order our lives.
2. Worship, which is the way in which we respond to that in which we believe; and,
3. Sharing, which is the way we express our belief in the giving of our time, our abilities, and our resources.

Anne Novak, lay parish assistant
Trinity, Milton, VT 05458

I believe a growing, effective stewardship to be a direct result of a growing commitment to Christ and our mission and call to be Christ-bearers. The focus then, to me needs to be on developing spirituality rather than on stewardship. I am turned off by a list of gimmicky, clever "ways" of doing or encouraging stewardship, because any level of stewardship, no matter how high, has no particular substance if it does not spring from authentic awareness of God, his abundant goodness in our lives and a growing, deepening commitment to mission. Until the people in the pews—and in the pulpit—are enabled by the ministry of the parish and diocese to interface with Christ's love in ways that are relevant to their lives, stewardship is a non-issue. This is the issue that is critical—do people meet and journey with a living Christ in their parish who challenges them by his unconditional love and acceptance? When they do, stewardship and evangelism will fall into place.

The Rev. Patrick H. Sanders
Church of the Atonement, 4945 High Point Rd. NE, Atlanta, GA 30342

Sacrificial giving to others of our money can be a powerful demonstration of how we feel about a totally giving God, and about our own ministry to ourselves and to each other. Such giving can deliver us from the idolatry of money.

We do not give to the church because the church needs us to. We give because we need to, since our own ministry includes each part of our lives, and our money is such a powerful force.

The Rev. Frank H. Clark
Trinity Church, 405 N. Madison, Pierre, SD 57501

The stewardship sermon should not be saved for Canvass Sunday but something that comes ahead of time, so that people can have time to think about what they are going to do. If we follow the lectionary and talk about the parables and other events that have to do with the stewardship of our possessions as they come up, it should not be a strange subject when we come to the time of our every member canvass.

The Rev. Kendrick H. Child
St. Matthew's, Main St., Lisbon Falls, ME 04252

We believe our growth in numbers and success in stewardship are related, not to any organized approach to this end, but rather to an understanding as a group, of God's call in our lives to carry out the great commission. Good stewardship is a by-product of successful evangelism and church renewal, and follows automatically and without effort, when people come to really know and understand the Lord and his mission for us.

The Rev. Philip J. Nancarrow
Church of the Transfiguration, Box 732, Ironwood, MI 49938

A congregation which has a fairly clear sense of what it is doing, and which believes what it is doing is right and good, has relatively little trouble with stewardship. The people in that congregation who accept and support the program which grows from or expresses a sense of purpose will offer their time, energy, and money to see the program fulfilled.

The Rev. Ronald L. Reed
Christ Church & St. Michael's, Germantown, 29 W. Tulpehocken St., Philadelphia, PA 19144

I must say that I not only have not been reluctant to talk about money especially in terms of stewardship, I have been enthusiastic in discussing money. I consider that money is the primary medium that human beings have to bring the Gospel to the world beyond themselves personally.

David P. Prescott, Chairman of the Stewardship Committee, Trinity Church, Princeton, NJ 08540

The backdrop for this effort is a general stewardship statement created by the stewardship committee. It was an attempt to open our thinking about stewardship and its consequences. The essence of the statement is as follows:

Trusteeship
God has chosen us, as a part of God's own creation, to participate in it. The creation is God's, not ours. It is given to us in trust, as stewards, to develop, use, enjoy, and share; to manage and protect for ourselves and future generations, in the furtherance of God's purposes—not our own. We can exercise our stewardship and share in God's creative activity in many ways: by giving our time, skill, and money to various enterprises; by caring for and tending our fellow creatures; by using natural resources responsibly; by working toward the improvement of the social order and the development of honest personal relations, a constructive community life, and a peaceful world.

Consequence
Faithful stewardship is an act of thanksgiving and caring for God's gifts and grace which helps free us from capture by earthbound concerns. A life of getting and having, of conforming our conduct to customs and expectations based on human values which ignore God's purposes, is indeed bondage to objects or position or "public opinion." A life of faithful stewardship, of sharing and caring, is service to God, defined by the ancient Collect for Peace as "perfect freedom." As we see as our priority the attainment of God's goals rather than our own we can become what we were created to be, free from debilitating and irrelevant choices and joyfully empowered to act as God's instrument in the world.

Pursuant to these thoughts, the Vestry adopted a statement relating to proportionate giving, which is as follows:

The philosophy of proportionate giving is an appropriate means of ordering one's commitment, goals, and life. It has proven helpful to each member of the Vestry, which has endorsed it as the guiding principle for the stewardship visits this fall. We commend it to you as well.

The essential elements of proportionate giving are:

that each person return to the parish a faithful proportion of his or her time, talent, and money in thanksgiving for the gifts of God;

that each person decide, after prayer and reflection, what his or her commitment will be;

that we all try to set some personal goal in financial giving and strive over the coming years to achieve it.

Proportionate giving encourages us to look at our needs and priorities freshly every year, so that our commitment genuinely reflects what we can and want to give. This philosophy may lead us to increase our pledges or, if necessary, to decrease them responsibly.

We feel that these two statements articulate a solid theological foundation for use in our Every Member Visit program.

The Rev. John T. Broome
Holy Trinity Church, Box 6247, Greensboro, NC 27405

The success of the EMC in 1978 and 1979 was due to several factors which enabled Holy Trinity to tell its "story"—problems of the past, needs of the present, and vision for the future:

1. Clear goals that were articulated and presented well.
2. A specific and thorough plan to accomplish the goals began five months before the EMC.
3. Attractive and eye-catching literature briefly and clearly

stated. We chose gold paper and red ink to set EMC literature apart from other parish mailings.

4. A positive approach to pledging that educated and motivated the parish.
5. The active leadership and support of the Rector and the parish staff.

The primary reason for Holy Trinity's successful EMC, however, was in presenting it in the context of faith and prayer instead of percentage increases and telling parishioners what they ought to do. Their decisions were in response to their serious consideration of Christian stewardship.

The Rev. George H. Martin
St. Luke's, 4557 Colfax Ave. S., Minneapolis, MN 55409

In the past few years we have focused on a pledge Sunday when we encourage people to come to church to present their pledges. Most important in the past *two years is our realization that prayer is at the heart of a canvass.* With credit to Terry Fullam, we now have a vigil on the eve of the canvass encouraging people (especially our parish leadership) to come to pray for the church and for guidance in their own giving.

The Rev. Michael R. Becker
St. Mark's, 1625 Locust St., Philadelphia, PA 19103

Our theology is simply this: that *we believe that one's stewardship is the best possible indication of one's personal commitment to Jesus Christ,* and that such committed giving frees one from the demonic hold which our money has over us and forces us to have a whole new set of priorities. This is so because:

1. Money is where most of us "are at"—it is the real center of our lives, and our true security. The incredible hostility which any stewardship program can produce is surely proof enough that to be parted from our money is a serious threat to most people.

2. True personal commitment, then, can come about in no better way than through the giving of money and being set free from the hold and power it has over us.

In reply to a remark of mine in a letter to him, Fr. Christian Swayne, of the Order of the Holy Cross, writes this to me: "What you say about pledging and personal commitment to Jesus is so right on. I think that if the Church didn't need money, it would have to take it anyway and then burn it, because it is so essential to give it. Certainly Jesus thought so, and said over and over again, sell all you have and give it away. We might as well give it to the poor, but the point is the giving away of it—not relieving the poor."

The Rev. Gray Temple, Jr.
St. Patrick's, 4755 N. Peachtree Rd., Atlanta, GA 30338

Since 1976 our stewardship program has attempted to embody what we regard as a straight biblical theology of money. We understand that to comprise the following aspects:

First, in terms of the old "time, talent, and treasure" disingenuity, we concentrate on "treasure." We assume that people's hearts follow their treasure. *We are addressing appeals for time and talent all year round.*

Second, we recognize that *money is essentially a spiritual force.* Nobody really understands it. Its symbolic value and consequent ability to complicate lives by its presence or absence is simply bewildering. Most people in our neighborhood experience those complications as some form of bondage, usually debt and irrational spending patterns.

Third, we find in the Old and New Testaments *much evidence that the Lord takes our use of money seriously.* He requires righteous spending, generosity to others, and the minimum of tithe to his work. In return he offers freedom from care and want.

He rescues us from bondage as we exercise the principle of "sacrifice," that is, of "making something holy." Sacrifice is applied to several difficult life situations in the Old Testament. To rescue us from anxiety about time, God requires the seemingly irrational gift of the Sabbath. To hallow child-rearing, God demands the dedication to himself of the first son. To sanctify and simplify interpersonal relations, God requires special conditions be attached to one—marriage. To sanctify commerce, God requires one year in each person's lifetime in which it is cancelled—the jubilee. And to rescue us from financial bondage, God asks that we make an irrationally large sacrifice—the tithe. In each instance, the sacrifice of the part allows God to hallow the whole.

The Rev. Clayton E. Crigger
St. Francis, 509 S. Rosemont Rd., Virginia Beach, VA 23452

Tithing is a confusing principle to many people. This is because they see only the "letter" of the law rather than the "spirit" of the law.

Obeying the former can bring a satisfaction with ourselves and make us judgmental of others. (That makes it feel like an obligation to be met and then dismissed.) It is a form of tokenism. Anyone can live on 90% of what they make. Most people spend at least 10% of their income on some venture that brings them contentment—be it recreational, educational, cosmetic, etc.

The truth God sought to teach was in the "spirit" of this law. He is very simply saying, "Return to me that substantial part of yourself that will help order your priorities when spending the rest of yourself. Make me the recipient of the 'first fruits' of your labors and yourself." It is a wonderful measure of to what you are committed.

My gift to God can in no way repay his generosity, but it is a way to say "thank you." One doesn't say "thank you" for anything they feel they rightfully deserve. We give our most profound gratitude when we realize we have been blessed with something very special and unconditionally given. This is the grace of God given freely to us; my response is simply to say "thank you" in the most real and significant way I can find every day that I live.

The Rev. James E. Folts
Church of the Heavenly Rest, 602 Meander St.
Abilene, TX 79602

Specifically concerning the stewardship of money, we offer the following thoughts. *We understand money to be nothing more than time translated into a negotiable form.* For instance, if I work at a job and am paid $5.00 an hour, I trade one hour of my life, the time given to me on this earth, for that $5.00. How I spend that $5.00 reflects then the value I place on my life, on that great good gift God gave to me. *We hold before our people the tithe as the traditional standard and norm for a Christian's offering.* To that end we teach that the tithe, or 10%, is the minimum goal toward which we each strive. To attain that minimum goal we encourage our people to become proportionate or percentage givers, and to increase that proportion each year until their goal is reached. And at the same time we do much to teach that the Christian's real responsibility and first responsibility as a steward is very consciously to render to God one hundred percent of all they have, in the sure knowledge that all that we have is from God and we are accountable for the use we make of one hundred percent of it, not just the 10% we return to him through the Church.

The Rev. James A. Corl
St. Paul's, 200 Jefferson Ave., Endicott, NY 13760

Our Theology of Stewardship.
    Genesis 1:1. "In the beginning, God. . . ." We give out of thanksgiving and we see everything we have and are as useable in God's service, all the time. We give to God; it is not important *through* whom we give, but *to* whom. It is important what the

act of giving does to the individual. The relationship between a person and his possessions is a mini-parable of his relationship with God. One purpose of a stewardship campaign is to build an awareness of God's total saturation into our lives. We raise the question, to whom are you giving, and what are you saying to him with what you give?

We reject the following theologies of stewardship:

a. God-has-nothing-to-do-with-it theology: avoid all mention of money except once a year.
b. Theology of sympathy: cry poor.
c. In-money-we-trust theology: Talk about money constantly.
d. Theology of comparison: Look at old St. . ! We could . . . if. . . .
e. Alma mater theology: Play on loyalty to the parish (to whom are we giving?).
f. Theology of modern tithe: 5% to God, 5% to philanthropy. God only cares about part of what we have.
g. Big brother theology: Scaring them with the unknown, otherwise known as the God-will-get-you theology. Make them feel guilty.
h. Save-'em theology: Implies that salvation is getting others to do what we want them to do ("we know what your stewardship should be . . . and if you want to be right with God . . .").
i. Cookbook theology: Using Bible to proof text. Bible is our God.
j. Theology of numbers: God will love you if you raise your pledge x %.

The Rev. Don L. Robinson
St. Mary's-in-the-Valley, Box 491, Ramona, CA 92065

Commitment is the key. I subscribe to the theory that when you get the man you get his money, and not the reverse. I never speak from the pulpit in terms of dollars, only of percentages. I stress tithing as the standard and not the end of giving. I constantly keep before my people the many causes worthy of our financial response above and beyond the bare requirement of 10%. Opportunities for additional giving are frequent.

The Rev. Robert L. Sessum
All Saints, 525 Lake Concord Rd. NE, Concord, NC 28025

From our biblical knowledge we are aware of the word "tithing"; that is, giving of one-tenth of all to God. In today's time and age, I doubt if many of us are anywhere near that figure, but we all could and can be working toward it. Out of sheer curiosity, why don't we look at the percentage we are giving. Take your pledged amount for this year, divide it by your total income (whether you do it before or after taxes doesn't matter).

Where do you lie in the biblical 10 percent standard? 1%, 3%, or even 4%? Why not try to move up a percentage or two this year until you meet the suggested tithe? Our needs are large, and your all-out support is a must.

SUMMARY OF STATISTICAL BASE FOR ABOVE INFORMATION

91 dioceses contacted

59 responded with names/places—total 264
  64.8 percent response

Of 264 names/places supplied,
74 responded with data
  28.5 percent response

By Provinces:	*Replies received*
Province I	4
II	10
III	8
IV	23
V	3
VI	9
VII	8
VIII	9
	74

74 replies broken down by communicant strength (adult membership) of churches

Communicants	*Replies*
100 - 199	19
200 - 299	12
300 - 399	12
400 - 499	11
500 - 699	10
700 - 999	3
Over 1000	7
	74

Chapter 6

And Now Down
to the Nitty-Gritty

Having attempted to describe some of the foundation blocks on which we build, we come now to the very practical problems of planning and executing the actual financial stewardship program in a parish.

There are three assumptions that underline what follows:

1. One of the keys to an effective program is disciplined and detailed planning. More messages are delivered during a stewardship campaign by nonverbal means than are ever "heard" by the words we speak. A poorly planned and conducted program will loudly proclaim over and over again, "It is not important!" "It is not worth your best!" "It should not command your support!" A carefully worked out plan of presentation is essential:
   - To achieve the best results, spiritually and financially
   - To develop credibility—that you know and are convinced of the value of what you are doing
   - To enable people to make a considered response to something attractive and compelling
2. In order to maximize the results, the actual financial stewardship program needs to run a minimum of four weeks and can profitably involve up to six weeks of the attention of a congregation. A one- or two-week effort will generally achieve a minimum result. The digesting of ideas and materials to be presented and the building of the spirit of enthusiasm and the desired level of parish involvement require time. The pot

needs warming before it will boil. Four to six weeks seem to work out best for the process to happen.

3. The support and intimate involvement of the rector is essential. What we are doing in stewardship is fundamentally a spiritual task with strong spiritual overtones and potential for parish and people alike. It is an opportunity for the spiritual leader of a congregation to have an impact on the lives of people where they really live in a way seldom available to him or her. Or, to put the matter in reverse, to say that what we are doing has spiritual substance and consequences for our members and then to conduct the program without major involvement from the rector, is to deny, nonverbally, the very message of our words. To be sure, there are many lay people who have both the skills and the spiritual depth to do everything I am suggesting, and to do it well. But it is the rector who is identified as the spiritual leader, whose intimate involvement creates the essential spiritual base and credibility that are needed.

On the basis of those three assumptions, let's turn now to the detail work.

In a *Peanuts* cartoon, Snoopy is pictured in a tree, deep in his Walter Mitty–style imaginings. He says, "Here's the fierce mountain lion waiting for his victim." Then Linus enters and Snoopy eyes him as his intended victim. He leers at him, poises himself, and then, with a scream, "Augh!" he pounces. But the leap to light on Linus's head is without effect. Linus doesn't even look up. Snoopy, crestfallen, simply rides his perch in Linus's hair, saying, "Somehow my attack seems to lack force."

It is at the point of attack that we now stand. How can we give it force to command the attention and provoke the response of the congregation?

The elements we need to put together include the following:

1. A clear understanding of our biblical theology about money and specific ways in which that understanding will be communicated

2. A detailed calendar of all events to be undertaken

3. A specific method by which canvassers are to be selected
4. A specific way of training canvassers
5. A specific way of assigning canvasser calls
6. A system detailing:
    a. the content and timing of preliminary mailings to the parish
    b. the content and timing of sermons, talks by lay people, parish meetings, etc., so as to build steadily to the time of pledging
    c. a system and time for preliminary canvasser calls on parish members
    d. all deadlines to be met by canvassers
    e. clean-up dates
    f. plans for a victory/thanksgiving celebration at the completion
    g. plans for reporting results to the parish membership

What follows in this chapter are some ways in which these things can be accomplished. Everything suggested here is subject to revision and adaptation to fit a variety of situations. It will, therefore, be offered in outline form for easy adaptation.

Assuming your annual stewardship program will cover five weeks, two calendars are suggested to run side by side.

A STEWARDSHIP CALENDAR
Organizational

Preliminary Steps:

Their tasks over the summer should include:

June 1: Select the stewardship chairperson or co-chairpersons.
    a. To select the specific theme and emphasis for this year, in consultation with the rector and/or stewardship committee
    b. To become familiar with and committed to the theology, the particular mechanics of your campaign and any specific stewardship problems peculiar to your parish

    c. To analyze the pledge profile of the parish, identifying active and inactive members, pledgers and non-pledgers, and any unique characteristics in the parish pledge profile

    d. To review and select, or write (which I recommend, where possible) the stewardship mailing pieces you will use

    e. To select the key canvassers (about 20 percent of what you will need), contact them and secure their agreement to serve as leaders

    f. To establish the stewardship calendar for that year, listing all major events planned

September 1: With the advice of the rector and using the 20 percent of your leaders as contact people, all canvassers are now selected and their agreement to serve secured.

September 1: All stewardship materials are to be on hand . . . pamphlets   pledge cards   posters   etc.

At the September vestry meeting: A complete review of plans, theme, materials to be used, and the calendar of events is presented for approval and support. Even if the preliminary planners are vestry members, such a presentation will have the effect of clarifying the plans, bringing the entire vestry into support of those plans, and giving the leadership a deadline toward which to work.

Mid-October: Parish stewardship training sessions: depending on numbers and circumstances, one, two or three identical sessions may be needed. It is strongly recommended that *all* canvassers be required to attend a training session. (See Addendum 2)

    When these preliminary steps have been taken, then you are ready to launch the program itself. The following is one way it has been done effectively.

    The communications calendar below is based on a five-week canvass, involving three Sundays.

THE EVERY MEMBER CANVASS
Communications Calendar

Week One:

Prior to this the stewardship leaders have been meeting to work on the program. Simple announcements about those meetings have alerted the congregation to what is coming.

1. In the first "official" week the *first mailing* to the whole parish is sent, announcing and outlining the details of the program. Such a mailing should include:
   - dates and places of all events
   - how and when pledges can be made
   - what the canvassers will do
   - titles and themes of sermons to be given
   - an invitation to participate in events
   - a request for parish-wide prayers for stewardship
   - an example of a prayer that could be used. (See Exhibit 1, Chapter 8, for an example)

   It should also feature a written statement on the basic theology of money, done with some imagination. (See example in this chapter)

2. The first canvasser call on parish families should be made in this first week also. This first call does not ask for pledges nor should any be accepted. In fact, pledge cards should not be made available to anyone, except in very special circumstances, until Pledge Sunday. This call asks for participation in the events of the weeks ahead. The first call has four primary aims:

   a. Introduces the caller to his or her families (this initial call can also be used to update parish records, gather needed parish information, etc.)

   b. Explains details of the program and clarifies any confusion

   c. Invites participation, offers transportation to these events, including Sunday services

   d. Encourages feedback on parish program

3. Initial canvasser calls can be made:
   a. Individually in homes, which is the most effective method
   b. In canvasser's home by his or her invitation—an evening coffee, dessert, party, etc. (informal social evening, low key invitation to participation)
   c. By telephone, a less effective method
   d. Writing a letter or note, the least effective method

Week Two:

1. Second mailing:
   a. Reminder of details as outlined in the first mailing
   b. More on theology—different tack, same message (See examples in Chapter 8)
2. First Canvass Sunday
   a. Sunday sermon based on the Church's missionary imperative (See examples in Chapter 8)
   b. Prayers for canvass in church
   c. A short service for commissioning of canvassers as part of the regular worship (see example in this chapter)
   d. Potential three–five minute talk by a leading lay person. This talk is (1) not a sermon nor (2) a presentation of the church's need. It is a witness by a lay person of how his or her family makes their pledge and how they feel about it. Lay sermons and pep talks about parish needs tend to communicate pressure and are usually counterproductive. A simple personal witness communicates experience and allows the listener to identify his or her own experience as well.
3. Potential parish meeting for presentation of ministry
   a. Evening session with supper
   b. Coffee hour session following morning services

Week Three:

1. Third mailing:
   a. Move from writing on theology of giving to ways Christians can consider measuring their gifts. An article on

   proportionate giving as a way to consider pledge (See examples in Chapter 8)
   b. Reminder of when and how to pledge
2. Sunday sermon on "Mission of the Church"
   a. Potential themes:
   • What is the purpose of (your parish name)?
   • Priorities for ministry in (your parish name). (One way to get at priorities is to ask yourself, your vestry, and/or your stewardship committee what would we do here if money were not a problem, i.e., if we had all we could spend? Such a discussion tends to open the mind and pull everyone's nose off the grindstone for a time.)
   b. Continued prayers for canvass
   c. Second potential lay person's witness talk (three–five minutes)
3. Potential parish meeting for presentation of ministry (See above)

Week Four:

1. Fourth mailing:
   a. Second article written on how a pledge best can be calculated. An article reinforcing the principle of tithing and proportionate giving as a way to consider a pledge, backed up by a chart detailing pledges based on income to which a percentage has been applied (See examples and discussion in Chapter 4)
   b. Details about when and how to pledge
2. Second canvasser call, by phone or post card, thanking families for participation in events thus far, including Sunday worship and encouraging attendance at remaining events, especially Pledge Sunday
3. Sunday sermon on "Giving"
   a. It should deal with giving as a spiritual matter, and deal with money and giving directly and clearly. Some inclusion of tithing and proportionate giving as a method (See examples in Chapter 8)

  b. Third potential lay person's witness talk (three–five minutes)—
4. Pledging can be done on this Sunday
  a. In church, following the sermon, while sitting in the pews
  b. All canvassers meet at church, after worship, for dessert and coffee. Canvassers receive names of their assigned families who did not pledge in church—to be called on *that afternoon.* Cards returned to central recording station by 6:00 p.m. (Note in this calendar three levels of communication designed to reach almost every family in the parish: the written word, personal caller contact, and the spoken word on Sunday. A breakdown in any one of these will cut out some who will not respond to the other two.)

Week Five:

1. Clean up all remaining calls
2. Don't allow it to get strung out—
   Lose momentum   Lose enthusiasm   Lose impact
3. Calls not completed can be turned over to a clean-up committee
4. Report results to date to the parish—important for parish interest and satisfaction

POST-CANVASS

1. After the five weeks, get cleaned up as rapidly as possible
2. Report results to the parish, a complete report to be given two weeks after Pledge Day with the final results
3. Celebrate completion on Sunday with thanksgiving and joy
NOW—Get at budget preparation.

GENERAL COMMENTS

If the life of a Christian depends, in part, on his or her giving
. . .

If the life of a parish depends, in part, on being able to support
salaries, program, buildings, outreach . . .

Then . . .

The fall financial stewardship program is one of your most
important functions.

And . . . it deserves your best shot.

SELECTION, CARE, AND FEEDING OF STEWARDS
(Some suggestions)

If your stewardship campaign is one of the major events of
your parish year, the results of which will largely determine the
extent of your parish program, and if your stewardship campaign is fundamentally a *spiritual* adventure, then who does
your stewardship calling and how they do it become significant
items.

Every parish will vary in how they select and train their
stewards, but the following suggestions may be helpful.

Selecting Stewards

1. Use your most active people regardless of how busy they are.
   The effort deserves the best. This is no time to select someone
   "to help them become more active in the parish."
2. Select the people who are most likely to be recognized by
   your parish membership as the real leaders of your parish
   life. Those already involved and committed to your parish
   life are the ones who will carry the most authenticity when
   they speak to others.
3. Select those who are already your most sacrificial givers.
   Experience and established commitment are the best mo-
   tivators in talking with others.
4. Select those who are able to recognize the value of a time
   schedule and the meeting of deadlines. Serious procrastina-
   tion on the part of stewards is a heavy weight.

5. Generally speaking, a ratio of one steward to seven families is ideal. One to ten seems maximum.
6. Do not hesitate to use women as well as men as stewards.

Assigning the Calls

Methods of assigning calls will vary considerably depending on the size and circumstances of a parish. While many methods will be effective, the point to be made is that *some method* be used and the matter not be left to a grab bag. Some suggestions may be helpful.

1. In a parish that is spread out, assigning calls by geographical neighborhoods may be your best guide.
2. Where feasible, calls should be assigned by approximate income levels, upper income people calling on upper income people, modest income people calling on modest income people, etc. These match-ups help communication, expectations, and effectiveness.
3. Stewards should be given the freedom to trade in an assigned call where there may be a personal conflict that would prevent a positive contact from being made.
4. Women may be assigned to any calls, but sometimes it is helpful to assign a woman of standing in the parish to call on other parish women who live alone.

Training of the Stewards

1. In order to ensure clarity of purpose and a united effort, everyone who is asked to make calls should attend a training session. In many places this is considered important enough to make it a requirement. To emphasize the importance of the task and to build some sense of stewardship team spirit, it is strongly recommended as a requirement.
2. The training session can be accomplished in one to one and a half hours. Where there are many stewards, two or three identical training sessions can be offered at different times.
3. The training session should include:
   a. A discussion of the theology, preferably led by the rector.

(An outline of the key elements in such a presentation follows.)

b. A review of expectations. What exactly do you expect of stewards, what are the deadlines, and how will what they do fit in with the rest of your program? A systematic review of your calendar will accomplish this. In this area, assume nothing and be detailed in outlining the stewards' tasks.

c. Some helps can be offered in very practical terms about methods of approach, i.e., the initial contact, later contacts, what you can say if . . . [the Church is criticized, the rector is criticized, a particular program in the Church is criticized; a person wants to give you a check for the whole pledge now; a person wants the card mailed; a person claims not to be a member, etc.]. Help should be given to stewards about how to respond to these and other situations you might expect to come up.

d. An explanation of the Stewards Commissioning Service, if you have one.

e. Leave time to handle the questions, anxieties, frustrations of stewards so they can be made as comfortable and confident in their task as possible.

f. Open and close your training session with your parish stewardship prayer.

AN OUTLINE OF A CHRISTIAN THEOLOGY OF STEWARDSHIP

I.

1. No one who lives can reasonably live without seeing life as a gift. We have done nothing to earn it. We simply have it.

2. For a religious person, the source of that basic gift and, indeed, the very earth in which our gift of life is lived out, is the Creator-God who made it and gave it to us.

3. For the Christian person, the greatest gift, as important as life itself, is the gift of Jesus Christ, through whose life, death,

and resurrection we can know and experience the love of God, here and hereafter.

4. In addition to these very basic God-given gifts, we have also been given a brain to think with, a body to work with, the raw materials of the world to create with, and countless opportunities in which to grow, learn, mature, and develop as people. While individuals will vary profoundly in what each one will make out of these gifts, basically, they are gifts given for which no one can claim responsibility.

5. Therefore, when we deal with stewardship, we are not dealing with ways to convince people to give of what they own, but the one basic need we all have to share of what we have been given. Stewardship involves everything we do all of the time. It involves our sharing of time, talent, and treasure—the traditional stewardship triangle. But it also involves our sharing of love, friendship, and concern, a less traditional stewardship triangle, and our sharing of these things in all our relationships, both in and out of the Church.

6. The specific claim of the Church on our sharing stems from our claim that it is the Church which is the major source of our understanding of this Creator-God, of the uniqueness of his Son, Jesus Christ, and of the power of the Holy Spirit that brings life to our life. It is in the Church, uniquely, that we can gather with other Christians to worship this God, to receive the Word and Sacraments, and to find fellowship and mutual support for living in concert with other Christians. Pledging to God through the Church doesn't pay for these things; it just allows them to continue to be, and to be available to all people.

II.

1. It is common human experience that there is a profound kind of satisfaction that comes to us when we share openly, that is not ours when we fail to share. We make a living by what we earn; we make a life by what we share.

2. Somehow, we know, without really needing to be told, that to share is more mature, qualitatively better, than not to share. There is a moral rightness about sharing, a moral wrongness about failing to share.

3. Somehow, as a built-in part of our human nature, we also know that it is essential to our happiness to be sharers. To share openly is to find a kind of well-being that those who do not share do not seem to have.

4. All these things are not necessarily true because the Church says so, but because they are part of the very fabric of our basic human experience.

III.

Stemming from these things, then, certain principles of an annual giving campaign emerge.

1. We need to give to God through many channels, of which the Church is only one. But basically, when we pledge to the Church we are giving to God, not to the Church.

2. We give to God through the Church out of thanksgiving for what we have been given, not in relation to the needs of the Church; thus, a giving campaign must be conducted *prior to* the formation of a parish budget.

3. If giving is an act of thanksgiving, then we need to consider giving not in relation to what we can spare after other things are cared for, but in relation to what we have been given; that is, in relation to our basic income.

A SERVICE FOR THE COMMISSIONING OF CANVASSERS

The canvassers come forward at an appropriate time during the service.

As the canvassers stand before the Rector, the stewardship chairperson says:

(Name of Rector), these members of our parish have been selected to be canvassers for the Church.

Rector: Stewardship is a part of the spiritual life of every Christian and every Christian congregation. You have been selected in our congregation to assist in the stewardship program of this parish. Do you accept this responsibility?

Canvassers: We do.

Rector: Are you ready to carry out your responsibilities faithfully and completely?

Canvassers: We are, with God's help.

Rector: Let us pray for these stewards and the stewardship program of this parish.

> Almighty God, the source of all that we have and all that we can hope for: Strengthen, we pray, the hands of these canvassers as they move among the members of this parish. Grant that they may be able to speak clearly and listen carefully as they call in your name. Help us all in this parish to respond openly to share ourselves and our substance truly as your disciples. And grant that we all may see the fruit of our labors in a parish ever growing stronger in your service; through Jesus Christ our Lord. Amen.

I commission you stewards of God and canvassers in the Church. Go forth in the power of the Spirit.

Congregation and canvassers: Thanks be to God.

Addendum I
On the Qualities of a Canvass Chairperson

Who should be selected to be chairperson of your Every Member Canvass? What qualifications should he or she have? The list below represents my own answer to those important questions.

1. A person who understands and is personally committed to the theology of money and its uses. Whether this person will be used as a speaker or not, his or her commitment will shine through and influence everyone with whom he or she works.

2. A person who is organized and able to live within the demands of a calendar and able to encourage others to do so as well. There are those who, by nature, seem to have little awareness of the "times and the seasons." And they are beautiful people. But, in the midst of an organized effort involving many people and many deadlines, such persons are unable to lead and will themselves be led only to frustration.

3. A person who is immediately recognized by the congregation as one of its accepted leaders. This acceptance, acquired through other activities, gives the campaign instant credibility as one of the important events in parish life.

4. A person who in his or her own family practices the discipline of proportionate giving. This is far more important in my view than that the leader be one of the largest contributors. Again, the commitment of the leadership will shine through everything that is done and said and be a positive influence on everyone with whom he or she works.

5. A person whose faith in Jesus Christ is apparent and growing. A committed Christian response is seldom offered where the leadership hasn't already made (and in their attitudes communicated that they have already made) such a commitment. Example always speaks louder than words.

6. A person who is able to have positive rapport with the rector. The need for a close, working relationship between these two is obvious.

Addendum II
Recruiting

I have suggested that the canvassers be required to attend a training session. If there are persons who are either unable or unwilling to attend such a session, you are probably further ahead to thank them and suggest that they might be better able to participate in another year. Such a stance, while it may appear a little arbitrary, does in fact deliver a solid message to your canvassers. It tells them that you believe in the importance of what you are doing enough to take the time and effort to plan such a session. It tells them that what you are inviting them to engage in is a community effort in which others are making similar commitments and will join them.

The same principles apply to all kinds of recruiting in the Church. So often, it seems to me, we go out asking for volunteers in ways that are not helpful. In looking for Sunday School

teachers, organizational officers, committee members, and sometimes even vestry members, we approach the task as though we
expect people to say no. We tell people things like, "The job is
not too difficult; it won't take much of your time or effort;
nothing much will be demanded or required of you, so why not
accept the job?" But, in so doing, what are we really saying to
the volunteer? Are we not saying, "The task is easy; anyone
could do it; neither you nor your skills are especially important;
what we really are asking for in this job is a warm, live body
to fill an inconsequential space." But suppose that we go to our
potential volunteers, having thought it all through, and say to
them, "We have a task that needs doing as well as we can get
it done. I'm asking you to help because you are the kind of
person and have the kind of skills that are needed. It may be
difficult at times; it will require a specific commitment of time
and effort from you, but it is a task worth doing and you are
the person we felt was best qualified to take it on." In this case,
what have you said to your volunteer? You have said, "You are
a person of real worth with something to give. We have thought
it through carefully and selected you instead of others. The task
is important and not just busy work, and it will challenge you
to get it done and satisfy you when it is completed."

It seems to me that the second approach affirms both the
volunteer as a person and the importance of the task. And,
beyond that, in the parish church it affirms the value of the life
of the parish and its total ministry to its people.

Addendum III
Suggestions About Canvassers' Calls

The initial contact you make as stewards will be an important
one. For most calls, it will be about the same time that the first
mailing piece has been received from the Church. Your task on
the initial call is to remind people of the details of the program,
to invite them to attend church, and to get acquainted with
"your families." Everyone's particular style of contact will be
different, but the following suggestions may be helpful.

1. Use your own natural style. A "canned" approach will seem artificial to those you are calling on and uncomfortable for you.
2. Tackle your easiest calls first. By the time you get to the less familiar calls, you will be an old hand at it.
3. Think about the people on whom you are calling. Consider their interests, their level of involvement in the Church, and any special circumstances you know about.
4. Get to the point of your call as soon as possible. This is not a social call, but it must be neighborly. Do not leave your family in doubt about the reason for your call. They are expecting to hear from you and most will welcome your contact.
5. Do not get drawn into controversy. If persons want to criticize the Church, *do not argue or defend.* Listen politely, draw out as much detail on the complaint as possible, and assure the family that it will be passed on to the right persons. Write down as much as you can right after the call so it can be passed on accurately.
6. Do not linger. When you are sure your message has been understood and any comments from your hosts have been heard, conclude the call pleasantly, expectantly, and expeditiously.
7. Thank them for their time and courtesy to you and reinforce your hope to see them in church next Sunday.
8. Pray before each call, asking God to help you be clear, warm, and pleasant in what you say and open to hear what is said to you.

Suggestions About Your Call

WHAT DO YOU SAY IF . . .

1. *Someone is critical of the clergy, the parish program, or someone or something about your parish life.*
   Respond sympathetically and openly. Do not argue or defend. For example, "I wasn't aware of the problem. Could you tell me something more about it so I can pass it on to whoever is involved?"

2. *Someone wants you to take their pledge now . . .*

   Thank them for offering, but remind them that for now what we are asking is their attendance in church and their prayers for the stewardship program. If they insist, tell them you have no pledge cards and invite them to church on Pledge Sunday, when pledge cards will be available for the first time.

3. *Someone doesn't want any more calls, but wants to be put down for "the same as last year."*

   We don't want to encroach on anyone's time, but you do not have any pledge cards and it would be most helpful if they could sign the card themselves in church on Pledge Sunday. If that's not possible, you would be glad to call in their home on or after that day to receive their pledge.

4. *Someone asks how much the budget is going up or what the Church needs, etc.*

   "The Church has a great many needs, to be sure, but we don't have a budget yet. Our real hope is that people will consider their pledge in relation to their income, their ability to share, instead of in relation to the budget. After our membership has pledged as they can, then we will develop a budget out of anticipated income." Remind them that this will be discussed in the parish newsletter and on Sundays, and invite their attention and attendance.

Chapter 7

Stewardship is More Than the Canvass

One spring I went on a short vacation trip to the western United States. On a Sunday I went to church in one of the prominent parishes in Southern California. The sermon that Sunday was an excellent, down-to-earth presentation of the theology of financial stewardship. Since I knew the rector and knew of his strong interest in stewardship, I was not surprised to hear him speak directly and plainly to the issues. What did surprise me momentarily was that it was April. I was further surprised to find that the parish was not conducting its annual stewardship program, nor was anyone being asked to pledge. Further, no suggestion was made that the parish was financially behind and pledges needed to be increased. It was simply a stewardship sermon delivered for the consideration of the congregation because the lectionary pointed to that as one possible theme for the preacher to pursue. I found myself refreshed by it and reminded once again of the assumption we have made from the beginning of this book. *Stewardship is a year-round concern of the Church.* Preparing for the fall canvass for financial pledges is only a part of a total parish stewardship program. Indeed, to do that alone, even if we do it well, is not to do stewardship adequately. I would go even further and suggest that without the support of a broader year-round emphasis, even the very best financial stewardship programs, while maintaining their theological/biblical appearance, will over the years degenerate into simple fund raising.

I know my friend in California well enough to know that he teaches stewardship year-round in many ways. I saw him doing it by preaching financial stewardship at a time when no pledges were being asked and nothing but deeper thought was to be provoked. That is one avenue of a year-round program. Clearly, stewardship is far more than money, and a year-round program will take us into many other areas of stewardship beyond the financial. So let's ask a basic question.

In its broadest terms, what is the heart of our stewardship before God? Is it not to know and to accept that God is the ultimate source of all that we possess and that as his stewards we are accountable for how we use what we have been given? The traditional words we use to describe "all that we possess" are the words "time, talent, and treasure." We would want to broaden that to identify, in addition, such things as our life and the gift of the earth and our responsibility to care for it. In what ways, then, can we, on a regular basis, teach and help people grow in our stewardship of all these things?

We need to say at the beginning that the most basic year-round stewardship is simply our awareness of it in our own lives. I find that the people I know whose sense of accountability to God for their lives is strong, naturally see their lives in terms of their stewardship every day. They make their choices about what they will do or not do, what responsibilities they will accept, even what social obligations they will take on, in terms of where they can best use the gifts that God has given them. Some of the people I admire most are people who live their lives on this basis. They are, for those willing to see, walking illustrations of year-round stewardship at its best. To be priests and to evidence such an awareness in our own lives is also, inevitably, to be teaching and illustrating stewardship all the time. Just as the most effective communications on prayer come naturally, verbally and nonverbally, from men and women of prayer, so the most effective messages on stewardship are delivered, year round, by people who are aware daily of the accountability of their lives before God. Would that we had an army of such

Christians to lead us! Would that all the teaching in the Church could be done by example! But, alas, we seem to lack both enough examples and the willingness to be led by such shining examples as we do have. So we turn to the harder task of having to teach by design.

To be effective, year-round stewardship teaching must be done consciously, that is, according to some plan and on a regular basis. Someone once said, "The best way for humans to be morally good is through some routine." I believe that to be true of the best way we learn as well.

Let me try to suggest three ways to teach stewardship year round that I believe have some substance.

I. Take the twelve-month calendar beginning in January, and you will find four natural stewardship teaching times that can be used.

a. *January—Choose a Sunday as near to the first of the year as possible.* Here is an ideal time to focus on the theme of *the stewardship of time.* Everyone, including the preacher, is conscious of the passing of time at the turn of the year. It is a time in the calendar when we also are aware that, for us, time is not inexhaustible.

How do we spend our time? If time is not infinite, it is important that we use what we have in ways that are responsible to ourselves, to others, and to God. It is important to exercise our stewardship by controlling how we use our time instead of allowing the passing of time to control us. If time is like money in the bank and we are only able to withdraw what is there under our name, then what we do with those withdrawals becomes important. How do we break up the time we are given responsibly between service to self, service to others, and service to God? To what extent, by the quality of our lives, do all these three overlap? The themes we could pursue are extensive, especially in a society like ours where busyness is seen as a virtue and the quality use of time is understood by only a precious few. Periodically and regularly thinking our way through our stewardship of time is a valuable and important enterprise. January is a good time to look at it.

b. *May—Choose a Sunday around Arbor Day.* The second stewardship emphasis naturally falls here on the theme of the *stewardship of the earth.* In no other way do we demonstrate our sense of partnership with God more deeply than when we plant a seed in the ground. In few other activities are we more dependent on the generosity of God expressed through the created order than we are when we set out a garden, plant a tree or a bush, or sow a field of grain. Consequently, there are few times when we can be made more aware of our responsibility to protect the gift of the earth and pass it on to the future as undamaged as possible as the spring of the year when we plant the seed once again. The themes for that Sunday could go as far afield into the subject of ecology as the ecological problems of any particular location dictate and the preacher's application of the Gospel permits. While this theme fits only indirectly into the trinity of "time, talent, and treasure," it is fast becoming, as it must be, a legitimate stewardship concern. It can best be opened up in the springtime.

c. *September—Choose a Sunday as near as possible to Labor Day.* This is the third natural occasion to focus on stewardship, this time on the theme of our *stewardship of talent.* It seems to stand now only as a part of the new American "long weekend." However, enough remains to provide a base on which we can look at our work—our vocations, professions, and jobs—and see them as a way to express our stewardship to God. One way to develop this theme is in terms of the way our work can be used in helping others, directly or indirectly. If you have wasted countless hours standing in a great variety of lines or on the end of many telephone lines "on hold," as I have, waiting for something that is not happening simply because of the inefficiency or lack of concern of the people you were waiting on, you probably have, as I have, a feeling that far more people need to see their work as helping work. More jobs are interrelated than we imagine. If I, by being efficient and concerned about the value of others' time, can enable them not to waste it, I have made a gift to them. The dollar value of what I do for or with them or the wage I receive for it is irrelevant to my stewardship in using it to help others. I'd like to hear someone develop that stewardship theme.

Another word-related theme could be the concept of producing quality work, whatever our vocation or job, as part of our worship of God, as part of our stewardship. Again the themes are almost without limit. Whatever the particular avenue of pursuit, Labor Day gives us a fall platform for such an emphasis.

d. *Late October or early November.* This time, of course, the focus will normally be on *the stewardship of money.* However, the financial aspect of our total stewardship no longer stands alone, but becomes a part of a larger concern, a concern that encompasses most, if not all, of our lives.

To pursue such a year-round teaching effort most effectively, these further suggestions, applicable to each of the four Sundays we choose in the year, may be helpful.

The sermon time is the best, most concentrated teaching time available in worship. If the parish is totally eucharistic on Sunday, while we are committed to a stated Gospel, we are still permitted some flexibility in choosing the Psalm, the Old Testament lesson, and the hymns. Any of these can be the source of sermon texts on the subjects suggested. If Morning Prayer is part of your Sunday worship pattern, there is the same flexibility in choosing Scripture reading appropriate to the theme.

In addition to the sermon, all other aspects of the service, insofar as possible, should be geared to emphasize the Sunday theme. This includes the choice of hymns, anthems, the use of special prayers on the theme, and at least one bulletin announcement directed to the theme.

If your parish has a time for adult education on Sunday, or a rector's class, here is another opportunity to spend some time exploring the theme.

The key to the congregation's understanding of the Sunday focus on an aspect of stewardship is that it be identified as such in the spoken word and in the printed bulletin. Many churches already emphasize these themes, perhaps even at the suggested times of the year. They will be seen by only a few in the congregation as stewardship themes, however, unless they are specifically identified as such.

II. *A second way to bring stewardship into the Church's program year round* is to undertake two Every Member Canvasses each year. The fall canvass for financial pledges, for most of us, is already in place. In addition, an Every Member Canvass can be conducted in the spring, this one for pledges of time and talent. It has long been my conviction that the financial canvass and a canvass for time and talent should not be conducted at the same time. I am aware that they are often done together. I am also aware that one reason we put them together is that pervasive feeling that asking for money is not quite spiritual enough and somehow asking for time and talent at the same time legitimatizes the other. Or perhaps we do them together because we, as the askers, are not comfortable dealing with the issue of financial stewardship directly and alone and want a broader platform on which to stand. I do not fault what anyone sees as effective in any particular parish. I would suggest that if this dual effort is not effective in producing substantial pledgings of time and talent, the motive for combining the two be examined and a separation be considered.

One obvious and substantial advantage to dual canvasses is that, without the financial pledge there to take precedence, the pleding of time and talent comes into sharper and clearer focus. While the spring time/talent canvass requires, in a sense, a duplication of effort or at least a significant effort to carry out, it will result in the uncovering of more pledges and, therefore, more available time and talent than anyone imagines. It also serves to spread the stewardship teaching opportunity into two distinct times of the year. Perhaps this is not a system to employ every year, but one that would be of great value every third year or so.

III. *The most obvious way to be sure stewardship is on the minds of your congregation year round is to use your parish mailing and/or your Sunday bulletin to write about it.* An aspect of stewardship (time, talent, treasure, ecology) could be the subject of the rector's column four times a year. In between, at a minimum of once a month, a short article could appear elsewhere in the mailing, either by a parish member or as a quotation from an outside source. The key to the effectiveness of such an approach is its breadth and diversity. Our temptation in writing about stewardship is either to focus too much on the financial aspects of it or not to touch that part of our stewardship at all and concentrate on the other stewardship themes. A predetermined schedule to cover all aspects of the stewardship theme is needed. It also becomes important for congregational understanding that the focus of any one article be identified as a stewardship focus.

Or you might like to do what my California friend did, *preach a sermon on the theme of our financial stewardship at a time other than when you are asking for pledges.* It might be a great surprise to your congregation. It might also do what it did for me, that is, take the financial stewardship message out of the "Oh, I must sign a pledge card" category and put it into the "Oh, let me think about that" category. No schedule for such a sermon need be devised. Let it happen when the Spirit and lectionary seem to lead.

One thing is certain. If, as someone once said, "stewardship is what we do, all the time, with everything we have," then stewardship is not only a proper but a necessary concern of the Church the whole year round.

Chapter 8

Resources and Examples

All of the following material has been used in actual parish stewardship campaigns.

RESOURCES A
Letters, Bulletin pieces, Mailers

Exhibit 1
To introduce the calendar and invite participation

(This piece is designed as a four-page folder and includes the material on pages 87 to 89 as a single piece.)

STEWARDSHIP NEWS

LOOKING AHEAD—The time has again arrived to begin thinking and praying beyond this year into next. For us at _____ Church, that means looking ahead and planning (and dreaming a little) about the quality, scope, and extent of our ministry here, and how we will be able to undergird that ministry with our Stewardship Pledges next year.

THE LEADERSHIP—A very able Committee headed by _____ and _____ has already set events in motion that will culminate in Pledge Sunday on November 7. A Calendar of Events is printed inside this folder so you can mark your own calendars and be in attendance at all these special occurrences.

A CALL FOR VOLUNTEERS—Of special note this year is our call for volunteers to help us. Usually each year, through the Vestry, we have selected men and women whom we have asked to dedicate their time and talent as canvassers. Because we don't know everyone who is able and interested in helping the church in this way, we are going about this differently this time. On the back page of this folder is a blank on which you may *volunteer* your services as a Captain or a Canvasser. Please use the blank and join us in this most important task. Thank you!

WATCH YOUR MAIL—You already have received the first of four small brochures, titled (YOU ARE THERE), describing an important aspect of the ministry of _____ Church and the motivation behind this ministry that we share together here. Please study these carefully. Also consider this truth: that through your stewardship gift to God through _____ Church YOU ARE THERE whenever this parish ministers in any way in any place, be it in our congregation, our city, our diocese, or our world. The brochures do not begin to tell the whole story of what YOU do and where YOU go through your pledged support of this great parish.

A Request for Prayers

Finally, we ask you to pray for our parish and for our Stewardship. If our pledges are the legs on which our ministry together walks, our prayers are the wings on which it can fly. So we ask you to join us in prayer that as God has blessed us, we in this wonderful parish church will be moved by his Spirit to bless others around us. A Stewardship Prayer that you might wish to use for this purpose is printed on the reverse side.

So We Ask You to Join Us . . .

. . . with your time and talent as Canvassers;
  . . . with your interest and concern by attending our stewardship events;
  . . . with your prayers, to put wings on our ministry together; and . . .
  . . . on November 7, with your pledge, to make next year another year of growing effectiveness in ministry both within our parish and to the world . . . all this in the spirit of Jesus Christ, our Lord.

Stewardship Calendar

OCTOBER 10 to 18—Search for volunteers to be Canvassers
OCTOBER 19 (5:15 P.M.) OR
  OCTOBER 23 (7:30 P.M.)—Training and orientation for Captains and Canvassers. (Workers attend *one*—1 hour.)
NOVEMBER 10 OR

NOVEMBER 14 ALL PARISH STEWARDSHIP DINNERS (To accommodate as many people as possible, we are planning two identical suppers and programs. Our families will be invited by alphabet, but anyone may attend either evening at their convenience.)

SUNDAY WORSHIP AND SERMONS:

OCTOBER 24—"The Imperative of Mission"

OCTOBER 31—"The Greatness of a Church"

NOVEMBER 7—"Now concerning the contributions for the saints . . ."

NOVEMBER 7—PLEDGE SUNDAY!!!

NOVEMBER 7 to 14—Canvass calls to be made.

NOVEMBER 21—Service of Thanksgiving to God for his empowering the ministry of _____ Church

A Prayer for Stewardship

Almighty God, our heavenly Father, you have given to us the many gifts of your love: a life to live and this good earth in which to live it out, and in your mercy you have given us the great gift of your Son, Jesus Christ; help us, we pray, to be bold in the sharing of these things with the world in which we live. Where we cannot go ourselves, inspire and direct us through our stewardship, to send others to go for us in your name. Bless our Every Member Canvass; and, remembering the account we must one day give, help us as people and parish to be faithful Stewards of your bounty; through Jesus Christ our Lord. Amen.

PLEASE RETURN THIS FORM TO THE CHURCH

_____ I will pray daily for our Stewardship Program

_____ I will work as a Canvasser

_____

Name

Street Address

City, State, Zip Code

Phone Number

Exhibit 2

STEWARDSHIP NEWS
On Motives for Giving

In II Samuel 24, David, the great Hebrew king, had been instructed, "Go up, rear an altar unto the Lord in the threshing floor of Araunah the Jebusite."

So David goes to make arrangements. The Jebusite farmer runs to meet his king, duly bows, and asks him why David should be seeking him.

David informs Araunah that he has come to buy his threshing floor in order that he might build an altar unto the Lord there. So the faithful owner, impressed by his king's selection of this site, waxes very generous. He not only offers to give the king the floor but also tells him to help himself to his oxen and wood and other necessary building materials. These were to be a gift from Araunah to David. Whereupon David makes this classic reply:

> "Nay, but I will surely buy it of thee at a price; neither will I offer burnt offerings unto the Lord my God of that which doth cost me nothing." So David bought the threshing floor and the oxen for fifty shekels of silver.

David's response is what first got me to thinking seriously about my own stewardship. How much was my offering to the Lord costing me? Could I say that I held to this higher way of thinking: that unless it cost something it is not really worthy of my Lord? Was my financial stewardship of the token variety, giving casually only because something was expected of me?

It was then that I began to think about, and to ask others to think about, proportionate giving as a way of giving that costs something. I invite you to begin thinking about this for yourself.

Pledge Sunday at Christ Church is November 7. As you look toward your response on a pledge card that day, I invite you right now to think about sharing a responsible percentage of your income as your pledge to God through this church.

Many, many people do this already. They have learned what David learned, that to live in harmony with their Lord they need to be responsive to him in a way that costs them something. For this is the startling truth: *It isn't worthy if it doesn't cost.* "I will not offer to the Lord my God of that which costs me nothing."

Exhibit 3

STEWARDSHIP NEWS
A STEWARDSHIP THEOLOGY

A good friend of mine in college was a great sprinter. He was on the track team, and our coach always said that he could have been an Olympic sprinter except for one bad habit—he always ran with his head down! He put his chin on his chest, his eyes on the track, and ran to many victories. But, he often *lost the big ones* because, under pressure, his habit got worse. The tougher the competition, the tighter his head would be locked to his chest, and the slower he would run.

Some of us live that way. Now and then we look up and ahead, but most of the time we live with our eyes glued to the things of the earth.

The Psalms speak both to my friend and to us. *"UNTO THEE DO I LIFT UP MINE EYES."* (Psalm 123:1)

A good place to begin checking our habits against that affirmation is in the way we think about our money. Having money in adequate amounts, and thus having the things we think money will buy, is an overwhelming preoccupation for many of us. A bold illustration of our preoccupation is to see the anger and frustration that we feel when inflation, which we cannot control, threatens to reduce the purchasing power of our money.

When we think about the sharing of our money with others through the Church, some of us still live with our heads glued to our chests. We have reached a plateau, and *there is no upward thrust to our giving.* We run with our eyes down so that we never get out of us the best that is in us. Vertical living, with our heads held high and focused on the things of greatest value, is immeasurably aided by vertical giving.

This is another reason why your church believes in and preaches proportionate giving. Those who follow this teaching, and there are many in this church who do, discover that it is one more practical way to lift up their lives to the Lord who is the source of all life.

As you look at the cross on the altar, notice that it would be a simple "T" shape were it not for the vertical point above the crossbar. The cross looks out of shape unless *the "upward thrust" is the dominant factor.* Is there upward thrust in our giving? As our income increases, does our giving increase proportionately? As we live each year with the Lord's blessings, does *the portion of our income* we are willing to share increase? Indeed, have you ever calculated the portion or percentage of your income you share in return for God's blessings? The percentage you share is yours to choose. That's a matter of mathematics.

That you consider sharing a responsible portion with the Lord through the Church is also yours to choose. That's a matter of your commitment and faith.

These eight great words of the Psalmist give us some guidance. They are words for every phase of our life, including our giving, to bring us life at its very best. *"Unto thee do I lift up mine eyes."*

> *PRAYER FOR STEWARDSHIP*
> Open, O Lord, the eyes of all people to behold thy gracious hand in all thy works, that, rejoicing in thy whole creation, we may honor thee with our substance and be faithful stewards of thy bounty; through Jesus Christ our Lord. Amen.
> (adapted from the Book of Common Prayer, page 329)

Exhibit 4

STEWARDSHIP NEWS
ON SACRIFICIAL GIVING

For many years now, you have heard that stewardship is *so much more* than simply raising money to meet the Church's need for support! Stewardship is the way you see your life in relationship *to a giving God*, and how, in all aspects of your life, you respond to God's tremendous generosity.

The *financial results* of our responsible stewardship is that the work desperately needing to be done by your church, and other charities that we support, in fact does get done.

But, the *motive* of our giving is not to meet these needs, but to meet *our own personal need* to respond to God's overwhelming generosity to us by becoming givers ourselves.

The Bible uses a word, often misunderstood, to help us see this more clearly. The word is *sacrifice*. In the Bible, to offer a sacrifice is to give *a portion* of something in order to make *the whole "holy."*

For example, to rescue us from anxiety about *all* of our time, God asks us to give a *portion* of our time and dedicate it exclusively to him. "Remember the Sabbath Day, to keep it holy." Giving him *one day*, freely, has the effect of hallowing *all* our days and *all* our time.

To enrich *all* of our relationships and give them quality, God asks us to accept special exclusive conditions for *one* relationship, the covenant of marriage. To be faithful in that *one* is to find enrichment in *all* relationships.

This is the principle of *sacrifice*, not seen as we often do, as a giving up of something but as a dedication of a part of something that enriches the quality of the whole.

In our *financial stewardship*, the same principle holds true. Money has the potential to rule our lives. Its ability to complicate our lives by its presence or absence is bewildering. To have adequate or abundant supplies of money is to·be tempted to value ourselves, *to see our self-worth in terms of our money* and our money alone. To be *without* adequate money is to be caught in another kind of bondage, the bondage of continual debt and sometimes irrational spending. But the basic bondage, in each case, is the bondage of self-doubt.

To rescue us from these potential (and, for some of us, actual) chains, God says, *"Make a sacrifice!* Dedicate a *portion* of your money to me, without strings, so the *whole* of your money, your *attitude* toward it and its *power* over you, can be redeemed."

That's why we speak of giving to God in terms of *proportionate giving*. The *portion* we set as our response to God's generosity becomes our sacrifice, through which, if it is reasonably set, God can hallow *all* of our money, indeed, all of our life.

So, when you consider your pledge, you are considering the quality of your whole life, its values and its standards. To dedicate a responsible portion of your income to God, *to make a sacrifice to God* that is proportionate, is to invite God, in the most concrete way we know, to hallow the whole.

That's a long way from raising money for the Church. It should be! The decision we make about our pledge, our giving, is one of the most important spiritual decisions we make.

A STEWARDSHIP PRAYER
Open, O Lord, the eyes of all people to behold thy gracious hand in all thy works, that, rejoicing in thy whole creation, we may honor thee with our substance and be faithful stewards of thy bounty; through Jesus Christ our Lord. Amen.
(adapted from the Book of Common Prayer, page 329)

Exhibit 5

MEDITATION ON A TEN DOLLAR BILL
On Setting Priorities

Before me on my desk I have just placed a $10 bill. It's a fascinating thing just to sit here and look at. For what that piece of paper represents probably occupies more of the thought and time and concern of most of us than any other single thing we know.

How to earn it, how to protect it from being stolen or wasted, what power we believe it gives us, what to spend it on, and that to which we will give it—these are all constant concerns of every day. Each of us will deal with these matters in our own way, but on one thing we can agree. Bury it in the ground, and it's just a piece of paper. But *use* it, and it has overwhelming power.

Money can become almost anything we want it to become. It can put new furniture in our living room, provide food for our table, put clothes on our back, and buy season tickets for your favorite team or for the Symphony.

It can also provide food to feed the hungry, or send a Christian missionary to the interior of Okinawa. It can be used to maintain a building where the Gospel is preached, the sacraments are celebrated, and where Christians gather to pray, to worship, and be of support and strength to each other in the faith. It can bring a doctor and a nurse and a teacher to northern Mexico, or place an unwanted child in a foster home where he or she can be loved and cared for. It can take a group of young people on a Christian retreat and a minister to a hospital when you are ill.

Or it can pay for a night out on the town.

We seldom have enough money to do everything we want. Thus, setting priorities for its use is one of the most important things we do. That's why Jesus talked about it so much. He knew that how we decide to spend our money is the basic key to what we really believe to be of value. That's why Jesus said, "For where your treasure is, *there* will your heart be also."

On November 7 each of us will be asked to make a commitment to God, a statement of our real values, on a pledge card.

Deciding what to put on that card is not a small decision.

Exhibit 6

HERE'S WHAT ONE PERSON SAID:
a lay witness letter (used by permission)

Dear Friends:

It is Every Member Canvass time. (Our rector) has asked me if I would write a letter saying why I give to the Church, and how I figure the amount.

I give because I want to give. The Church was not built by me; it was here and I grew up in it. That was lucky for me, because at a time of crisis in my life, when "everything that was nailed down was a'coming loose," I could not have survived if the structure of the Church had not been there to support me. The Church and the teaching it has preserved helped me to make sense out of my situation and gave me hope.

The Church is unique in that it continues to live because people freely give to it, and it exists only to give back freely. I want this to go on. I don't want the Church to die. It is here for me and I want it to be here for others.

Now, how do I go about determining how much I give? I consider the tithe—the tenth part—as a *minimal* response for me, just for *life!* I get more than a tenth out of life, and when I think of all that others have given me—things money can't buy—I get to feeling that a tenth is a rather niggardly response, in money.

It isn't hard for me to give that much. It doesn't hurt me, and it isn't a "sacrifice," because when I *really think* about where my money goes, I know that I spend quite a bit on things I don't really need, things I might even be better off without. Aside from figures (EMC's are loaded with statistics, budgets, before and after taxes, ad infinitum), I simply cannot live a life that isn't shared; I really cannot enjoy it.

Could it be that the miracle of the loaves and fishes was *possible* because one small boy shared what he had? Could be.

Exhibit 7

STEWARDSHIP NEWS
PROPORTIONATE GIVING

DURING THE PAST TWO WEEKS, in church and in a variety of printed pieces sent to you, we have tried to say some important things about our Stewardship. We have said that whenever the Church offers its ministry in our parish, our city, our diocese and our world, *you are there*, too, ministering through your stewardship gift. We have suggested the necessity of our continued and increased giving outside Christ Church, as well as discussing some of the needs within the parish.

AND NOW WE COME TO CONSIDER the pragmatic question: how can I be responsible to God, to our ministry in Christ Church, and to myself in my giving?

THE ANSWER LIES in the principle called *Proportionate Giving*. Simply stated, it works like this:

ENERGIZE OUR MISSION

Take what you have, i.e., your income, and make a conscientious return to God out of that income. Commit yourself to share a worthy portion of your income with him through your church.

PERHAPS IT'S BEEN A WHILE since you measured your giving. You can figure it out very easily. For example:
  . . . if your income is $10,000 and your pledge is $2.00/week, it should help you to know this represents @ 1% of income;
  . . . if your income is $15,000 and you pledge $8.50/week, this represents about 3% of income;

. . . if your income is $30,000 and you pledge $24.00/week, this represents about 4% of income;

. . . if your income is $6000 and you pledge $3.00/week, this represents about 2½% of income.

SHARE YOUR SUBSTANCE

PROPORTIONATE GIVING allows you to keep your pledge between you and God. It makes it a matter of the giver and his or her relationship with God.

TO PROVIDE SOME STANDARD to go on, the following is generally agreed to be true:

A 3% gift is the beginning of Proportionate Giving.

A 5% gift is the modern tithe.

A 10% gift is the biblical tithe.

Many Christians begin their giving with a modern tithe, i.e., 5% of income is given to the Church and 5% to other charities of their choice.

MONEY
MAKE, SAVE, GIVE
ALL YOU CAN

WHATEVER PERCENTAGE YOU MAY BE ABLE TO CONSIDER, *Proportionate Giving* is the way:

to be Christian in our giving;

to be honest with ourselves;

to be faithful to God;

to empower our ministry together.

Exhibit 8

A MESSAGE OF IMPORTANCE
FROM THE RECTOR
On the Meaning of Riches

Recently, someone telephoned me to ask if our parish could respond to a sudden and legitimate need. They asked for a sizable amount of money. I said that we were able and willing to do part of what was needed but could not do it all. The silence on the other end of the line was then followed by the comment, "Oh, I thought yours was a rich parish."

Indeed, we are a rich parish, rich in the Spirit, rich in the commitment of our people to Christ, rich in the enthusiasm with which we go about our ministry. And yes, we are rich in dollars given by dedicated people.

And we are rich in another way too, a way that tends to keep us poor. Our commitment to be a live, vital parish, evangelically, educationally, pastorally, and in outreach is deep and extensive.

We spend the gifts we receive carefully and effectively, and every year we also spend them fully, down to the last few dollars, to arm our ministry with strength and to make our work in Jesus' name sing "Gloria" to God.

Of course, we could do fewer things in our parish and save some money. We could curtail our outreach. We could become an average parish with an average program and we could have money in the bank. We could, indeed, become a poor parish and be a rich parish dollar-wise.

But God calls us to a different richness. Jesus' words, "Whoever would save his life will lose it; and whoever loses his life for my sake and the gospel's will save it," have great meaning to me. We are called to give our life, to throw ourselves into ministry as much and as well as our human and financial resources will allow. That makes us a poor, needy parish some-times dollar-wise, but rich in every other way.

I believe that you want this parish to be rich in this way. And that means we will always be poor, always in need of more gifts, and more people, and more dedication.

And because I know and believe that, I also know that you will join me on Loyalty Sunday, ready as I will be, with your increased and dedicated giving, to keep us rich and help us become even richer in the things that matter most.

Yours in his Name,
(Rector's signature)

Exhibit 9

A SAMPLE VESTRY STEWARDSHIP STATEMENT

We are all disciples of our Lord and Savior Jesus Christ by our Baptism. Because each of us is a unique person, we all express our discipleship uniquely, in an almost infinite variety of ways.

One common way all of us live out our discipleship daily is in the privilege and responsibility we have to administer and use the tremendous gifts of time, talent, and treasure we have been given and continue to be given by God. The way we think about and decide to use these gifts is called our Christian Stewardship.

As Christian stewards, we recognize God as the Giver and see ourselves as the receivers of God's gifts. We further recognize that our spiritual health and the quality of our Christian commitment is most concretely measured by the ways we use and share what we have been given. Christian Stewardship has the power to help us see where our values lie. A faithful stewardship response has an equal power to help us realign our priorities and values and thereby help us live out our commitment to the Lord more deeply.

In terms of our financial gifts and resources, we know the best way to express our commitment to the Church and to the Lord of the Church is by freely offering a prayerfully thought-out portion of our income, as we receive it, to God through the Church. This is called proportionate or percentage giving. The biblical standard of our proportionate giving is the tithe.

When we, individually as members of the Church, respond out of our gifts to God the Giver in this way, we have experienced, at least, these two results:

1) A great sense of satisfaction is ours because we have responded in our discipleship and to God's call faithfully and thoughtfully.

2) As the Church, all of us together in Christ's body are enabled to carry out our worshipping, pastoring, teaching, evangelizing, and outreach mission in and to the world most effectively in and from this place.

RESOURCES B

Examples of sermons that could be used in accordance with suggestions in previous chapters. All the sermons have been used by the author in his own parish.

Exhibit 10

"The Imperative of Mission"
Stewardship: Mission Emphasis

"Go therefore and make disciples of all nations, baptizing them in the name of the Father and of the Son and of the Holy Spirit . . ."

This morning here at Christ Church we are beginning our annual Stewardship Program. It is the beginning of our consideration of our giving to God through this church. For the next two weeks we will try to think about what our giving can do for ourselves and for the ministry of Christ Church. And specifically this morning we want to look at our outreach giving. Next week we will look more directly at Christ Church and our ministry here. On November 7th every family in this parish will be invited to make a financial commitment to God through this church next year.

So we begin where I believe we need to begin, thinking about ourselves as missionaries.

In the twenty-eighth chapter of St. Matthew's Gospel Jesus speaks the last words he will speak to his discples while he is yet on the earth. For forty days he has been with them as the Risen Christ, leading them, teaching them all the things they needed to know. Now they are together for the last time out on a hillside in Galilee. They worshipped Jesus there. Then, as though to underline the single most important thing that they are to do, Jesus says, "Go therefore and make disciples of all nations, baptizing them in the name of the Father and of the Son and of the Holy Spirit, teaching them to observe all that I have commanded you; and lo, I am with you always, even unto the end of the age." And then Jesus is gone from them for the last time in human form.

Down through the centuries these words of Jesus have echoed in Christian pulpits, in the minds and hearts of Christians everywhere. It is our commission. It is our reason to be Christians. It is our reason to be a Christian Church. "Go ye therefore into all the world."

It has been said that this commandment of Jesus is both the greatest glory of the Christian Church and our greatest shame. It is our glory because in response to that command we have gone out to preach the Gospel in Jesus' name to virtually every corner of this world. Some of the great heroes of world history are heroes because of their response to this command. It is also our shame because in response to that command our missionary outreach efforts have too often been timid, weak, ineffective, sometimes even absent, in the name of Jesus Christ.

Once again we face that command here at Christ Church as God's people. This morning I'd like to suggest some things that might help us consider it here.

The first is this: In the past several months it has been my increasing conviction that seldom in world history has the need for a Christian response to the world been so great as it is in our time.

Perhaps it is simply that we know more about the world than generations before us knew. Television, newspapers, magazines bring the world into our living room virtually every day. What we see is a world in turmoil. We see a world that is starving for food. And, yes, I believe we are seeing a world that is starving to hear the Good News of God's love.

Recently I was reading a series of articles about the world food crisis. Among the alarming facts that I read were these:

There are forty-six million human beings on the earth this very day who are threatened with death by starvation.

There are some ten million people who already have or will die of malnutrition this year, about 65 percent of them children under the age of five years.

To make matters worse, the world energy crisis has put the price of fertilizer out of the reach of most of the farmers who desperately need it in the underdeveloped nations of the world. It was estimated in this reputable article that one ton of fertilizer missing, because it cannot be bought, reduces the average crop yield in an underdeveloped nation by ten tons of edible food.

Now we have all read things like that. Quite frankly, while I did read those things with a twinge, I did not make much genuine response to them until I read two more things.

Senator Mark Hatfield gave a speech in the United States Senate some months ago urging our Government to respond to world hunger. When the speech was finished he invited the Senate to lunch. The menu on that day in the Senate dining room consisted of the following items:

Two ounces of grain millet, one boiled potato about the size of a Ping-Pong ball, one wedge of onion, and one-half cup of cold tea. That's all there was. It measured sixty-seven calories. That, the Senator said in this dramatic demonstration, is what one-half of the world's population eats in one whold day's ration of food.

Even that didn't bring it to me as forcibly as it should have until I read this. A United Nations Health Team went into the little African country of Chad to innoculate children against diphtheria. A father of a small child refused to allow the shot to be given to his starving son. The Health Team was astounded and demanded some kind of an explanation. This is what they heard. "My child will die of starvation," the father said. "Diphtheria is a faster, more merciful death than starvation."

Well, with that I could no longer put the problem aside as interesting and really too bad, but as not touching my life. Since then, whenever I have felt confused or overwhelmed by the problem of world hunger or what we might as Christians do about it, I have thought about that father. Then I know that we must do more than simply bow before the immensity of the problem.

There is another perspective in which we can see that kind of problem. Someone once thought about the world and reduced it to a village of 1,000 people. He wrote, "If the world were 1,000 people there would be . . .

"Sixty Americans, and 940 representing the rest of the world.

"The Americans would possess half the income of the world, with the 940 others dividing the remainder.

"The Americans would have a life expectancy of about seventy years, the remainder less than forty years on the average.

"The Americans would have fifteen times as many possessions per person as the rest of the world combined.

"The Americans would be well fed. Most of the other 940 would be hungry most of the time.

"The American families would be spending at least $500 a year on luxuries and entertainment, but less than $4 per year to share their blessings with the other people of the village."

It was Jesus who said, "To whom much is given, of him much shall be required."

"Go therefore into all the world."

It is not simply physical hunger to which I believe we simply must respond in our time. It is the spiritual hunger of the world as well.

Some years ago a seminary classmate of mine went to Liberia as a missionary. When he returned he came to a small church just fifteen miles from where I was serving in Minnesota. It happened that we shared the funeral of a four-year-old boy together. When we were finished at the graveside he told me this experience. When he first went to Africa, on his first visit to one of the villages he saw a woman sitting in a dusty street, crying as though her heart would break. He asked his African helper and guide what it was about. "She has been doing this for the past three months," he said. "She comes at sunup and stays until sundown weeping like that. Three months ago she lost her four-year-old son." And then the African guide said this: "As a pagan she has no hope in God beyond the grave."

We compared that to the family we had just left who mourned their four-year-old son as well. At the graveside he had read St. Paul's words, "For we would not have you be ignorant, brethren, concerning those who are asleep, that ye sorrow not even as others who have no hope. For if we believe that Jesus died and rose again, even so then also them who sleep in Jesus will God bring with him. . . . Wherefore comfort one another with these words." And while those parents had cried too, they had heard those words and they had cried in faith and belief.

I don't need to ask you about the difference. You and I both know it to be the difference between hope and despair, between the promise of heaven and a living hell. And what made the difference? The knowledge of the Gospel against the absence of the Gospel—that makes all the difference in the world.

And Jesus said, "Go ye into all the world and preach the Gospel."

Seldom in world history has the need for a Christian response to the world been so great as it is in our time.

But there is another side of the Christian missionary effort as well: a more hopeful, more positive side. And I need to tell you a story about that also. It is about a man whose name is Charles.

Charles in not an American. In fact, until recently Charles was not even a Christian. Charles lived in a small village in Okinawa. Everyone in the village was a friend to everyone else. Charles had always made friends easily. That is, until his face began to change. You see, Charles contracted the dread disease leprosy. Suddenly, Charles had no friends, no family, no home, and no place to go. He became a social outcast and a statistic on the list of those with an incurable, contagious, and terminal disease. Charles had seen leprosy before. He knew it spelled the end for him. He knew himself to be a man without hope.

That's when he met someone they called Father Keshei. Keshei Tanahara was also a leper. But Father Keshei was a Christian and a priest of the Anglican Church. Because Keshei was a Christian and a leper, he established a compound in Okinawa where lepers could come and live and be accepted. Father Keshei brought Charles there. There Charles was introduced to Someone Else, Someone who cared about the outcast and the sick, Someone who had said, "Come unto me, all ye that are weary and heavy laden, and I will give you rest." Charles met the Lord Jesus Christ in and through Keshei Tanahara. Charles still has leprosy and he probably always will. But Charles also has a place to be, a place both here and hereafter, for Charles is now a Christian.

Keshei Tanahara also has a place to be and a work to do in the name of the Lord. And he has, because here at Christ Church, halfway across the world, a body of Christian people who have never been to Okinawa and never seen Father Keshei but who hold the same Lord Jesus, every month pay Keshei's salary. We do, and will continue, because his is one of the faces of Christian missions that we must respond to in our generation.

The words are so familiar. They are our reason to be, our commission as a Christian Church. Without them we are little more than a club gathered. With them, we, with thousands of others who accept the Lordship of Christ, are the hope of the world. For we can still hear Jesus say, "Go therefore and make disciples of all nations, baptizing them in the name of the Father and of the Son and of the Holy Spirit, teaching them all that I have commanded you; and lo, I am with you always, even unto the end of the age." Amen.

Exhibit 11

"From Maintenance to Mission"
Stewardship: Raising Missionary Sights

Beginning today, and continuing for the next three weeks, here in our parish, we will be engaged in our Every Member Canvass program. Because of our Building Fund, which very properly has had a primary claim on our energies and resources in the past three years, we have not attempted a full-blown Every Member Canvass for three years. With the Building Fund's being completed this year, and if all goes well these last three months, being completed successfully, we need now to turn our attention to our support of the program of the Church, nationally, in our diocese, and here in our parish.

To help us all consider this as wisely as possible, we are going to do several things in the next three weeks. Each Sunday a layperson, a leader in our congregation, will speak on some aspect of our parish life. In addition, each week specific information will be printed and included in the Messenger for you to read and consider 'at home. All this will come to a climax on Sunday, November 7th, when every family in the parish will be invited to make their financial commitment to God through this parish. On that day, immediately following the sermon, while we remain in our pews, an opportunity will be given to make your commitment to God on a pledge card. Those cards will then be gathered and offered to God on the altar. For those who do not pledge during our worship, on that afternoon other parish members, men and women, will go out to call in our homes to talk about the Church and to receive our pledges for next year. We hope that by evening we will be substantially finished, so we can then turn to translating the financial commitments we have made into a budget for our parish.

Also in these three weeks, our sermons will be given to a consideration of the Church, where it is, where it ought to be, and how we can best be a part of that. This morning we want to think about the Church beyond our parish. Next week we will try to speak specifically about our parish. On November 7th we will be considering "The Subject Jesus Talked About Most."

So this morning we begin all that under the title, "From Maintenance to Mission." The text, if indeed a text is needed, is an old friend. From St. Matthew's Gospel, chapter 28, verses 18–20, "And Jesus came and said to them, 'All authority in heaven and on earth has been given to me. Go therefore and make disciples of all nations, baptizing them in the name of the Father and of the Son and of the Holy Spirit, teaching them to observe all that I have commanded you; and lo, I am with you always, even to the close of the age.' "

These are the closing words of St. Matthew's Gospel. As far as we know from the Gospel record, these are the final words spoken by Christ before his ascension. They are the most direct command of Christ to those who would be his followers. "Go ye therefore into all the world and preach the Gospel."

In our context this morning I'd like to begin with a very particular observation with special meaning for our parish. The command to "go forth" comes at the end of Jesus' ministry. The command to go into all the world is given only after three years of experience, of intimate fellowship, of learning, of growing in discipleship. Indeed, how else could it be? If the command is to go out and teach, then those who go out must first learn *what* to teach. If the command is to baptize, then those who go out to baptize must first know what baptism means and why it is so important and even how to communicate that meaning and importance to others. If, indeed, the command is to make disciples, then those who go out must surely be deeply convinced about him whose disciples they are, him to whom they would lead others by his command. Before you can "go out" you must have some base of knowledge and commitment to go out *from*. Jesus knew that and, I believe, deliberately withheld the command "to go forth" until these early Christians were ready.

Learn, grow, develop—then go out into all the world. That seems to be the pattern of the Scripture.

Now I don't want to push that too far, but as I look at our parish in the past five years, without really knowing it consciously, what we have tried, and tried very hard to do in these years is to build something here to go out from. Christian faith moves from a solid core, a solid commitment to a wider circumference, a missionary effort. What we have spent most of our time and energy doing in these fives years is strengthening that core. Our membership in five years has almost doubled. Our available and usable building space has tripled. Over 140 adults in this congregation have been involved in substantial Bible study. Attendance at worship on Sunday has expanded from an average total of 125 or 130 people to what you see today. In the process of these and many other things, by the blessing of God, the core, the commitment, the knowledge of this congregation has grown. To borrow a phrase from commercial advertising, with grateful hearts we can say of Trinity Church, "You've come a long way, baby."

That observation is of value only as it is followed by a second observation. The fellowship and learning and deepening of commitment that Jesus required of his disciples before he sent them forth, were all provided primarily so the time would come when he *could* send them "forth into all the world."

When you read the Scripture, there is no question that these apostles were being prepared for something. The day will come, you clearly assume as you read, when the teaching and the preaching and the healing tasks which belonged to Jesus will belong to them. They are being prepared, being readied to become his feet and his hands and his mind and his mouth to the world. That time came just before his ascension. He tells them, "Everything we've done together is for this. Now is the time. Go ye therefore into all the world."

Now again I don't want to push words too far, but at least it appears to me that there is a striking parallel in the recent history of this parish. We have spent time learning and growing and deepening our life as a parish. We still have a long way to go. But the time has come when God may be saying to us, "Everything you have done is for this. Now is the time. Go ye therefore into all the world." The time has come for us as a parish to begin seriously thinking of how we can shift our weight from maintenance to mission, from maintaining the core to being missionaries on the circumference, from what we can do for ourselves here to what we can do out there. Jesus withheld his command "to go forth" until his apostles were ready. Is it possible that God might now be saying to us as a parish, "You are ready. Go ye therefore into all the world."

That leads to a second observation. The world we are to "go forth" into isn't the same as it used to be. In a former generation, or even at the beginning of my generation, these words were filled with a multitude of familiar images. The commaned to "go forth" was acted on then by sending men and women to build a dispensary and mission chapel in the lowlands of India, or by sending a missionary and a teacher to start a chapel and a school in the interior of China. To "go forth" was to go into the hill country of Japan or the river country of South America or the coastal plains of Africa, to be the first to preach the Gospel to a pagan world. To be sure, that kind of mission work still goes on and needs our support. But in our generation these images have dramatically changed. They have changed because the world has changed.

For example, thirty years ago the most active, productive centers of the Christian faith were in the big cities. There is where the big churches were, in the heart and core of the city. There is where the power and the outreach of the Church was generated. But in thirty years all that has changed. With few exceptions the big church buildings downtown remain, but the people are gone out of them, moved to suburbia or into retirement and not replaced. In their place have come a new breed of people—low income, marginal, multiracial groups that surge into this forgotten inner city and must be ministered to.

Just to make a numerical comparison: in the suburban villages of Excelsior, Shorewood, Greenwood, and Deephaven, covering about seventy to eighty square miles, there are about 15,000 people. To serve these people there are 15 churches staffed by twenty-two professional clergy. By contrast, within a ten-block area surrounding Gethsemane Church in downtown Minneapolis there are also about 15,000 people. In homes where one family once lived, now ten families live in two- and three-room apartments. They live above stores and shops and in back apartments. In this area, besides Gethsemane Church, there are only two other churches of any consequence still active. Between the three there are now seven clergy and two lay workers.

John Weaver, one-time Dean of St. Paul's Cathedral in downtown Detroit, put this shift in missionary needs well when, at a conference, I heard him say this: "Prior to my first visit in Hawaii I used to pray for the missionary clergy of the area. But, once in Hawaii and living in its loveliness, I began to pray instead for the inner-city clergy who work in grime and filth and dirt to redeem the poorest of the poor. Do not misunderstand me," he said. "Hawaii needs our prayers, but for heaven's sake let's glamorize the real missionaries of our day. If any group needs our prayers and support, it's the inner-city church."

The missionary world of the Church is changing and that's one of the changes.

There are more. A few years ago the college campus, for example, was an ivy-covered world of academic pursuit and social convention. Now one hardly needs to be told that the ivy has been stripped away and the campuses have become the testing ground for freedom without restriction, for a large portion of the drug culture, and for whole new life styles that challenge the imaginations of most of us to understand. *Playboy* magazine, for example, the current national publication advocating male chauvinism, sexual freedom, and the satisfaction of the body over the satisfaction of the spirit, has a mailing circulation of about 300,000 copies a month. Of these, slightly less than forty percent are mailed to college and university addresses. Beyond all this, the explosion in knowledge, in the social sciences, and in technology has its greatest exposure on the campus. Often—significantly often—these things are offered to the student as an alternative to the student's religious faith.

The fact that these voices, these influences, are strong on the college campus is not all bad. It only becomes bad when other voices, like the voice of the Christian faith, are not heard, or heard so timidly as to have no influence at all.

The voice of the Church will only be heard as churches like ours see that we have a missionary stake, a missionary task to do.

There are other things too. Nursery schools are needed in parts of the city where mothers simply must work. Family training programs are needed in places where the disintegration of family life is most destructive. Counseling services are essential where counseling is desperately needed. The list could be made as long as we want. But the point that we want to make is that the world we are commanded to go into has changed. The image of the half-naked, smiling African black boy with his front teeth missing or the Oriental family in their coolie hats needs to be replaced by new images. Now we must begin to see children playing on dirt heaps and junk piles in the middle of the city; and families of seven and eight people living in spaces smaller than our garages; and students assaulted by every stimulus available except, far too often, that of the Christian faith. The world we are commanded to go into isn't the same world it used to be.

That leads us to make a final and very brief observation. If, indeed, we are commanded "to go forth," then how do we do that?

Somehow, we need to begin thinking of going forth as people. We are people, many of us, with real skills and training that can be used, can be offered to those who are in need. When Christ says, "Go ye therefore," we need, as people, to begin asking, "What can I do and where can I go with my skills?" Certainly, there are many more places needing skills, needing people, than there are yet people offering those skills.

Where we cannot go ourselves we can equip others to go. That is partly what our giving in the Church is all about. The world is changing. The places where Christian people need to go, need to be sent, are changing. But the command has not changed. Still he says to us, "Go ye therefore into all the world and preach the Gospel." And we must respond in every way we can.

Exhibit 12

"A Statement of Priorities"
Stewardship: Presenting the Church's Budget as Ministry

In the past two weeks the church newsletter and the mail going out from this church have begun to take on a different look. This is the time when we need to look at our stewardship of money in the Church.

In many places of which I know, this necessary emphasis, coming as it does once a year, begins to bring worry lines across the brows, and that pinched, mildly painful look that centers in the corners of the mouths of church members. The Annual Stewardship Program of the Church is thought by many to generate the same feelings that were generated when the Victorians of several generations ago thought about sex. For them sex was somehow necessary but not very nice. So stewardship, in some places, is received as necessary but not very nice.

I say in some places, because one of the joys of Christ Church is that that is not our stand. We are—we have learned to be and we are—enriched because we are a responsive, generous congregation. Because we believe so deeply in your generosity, we are doing our canvass a little differently this year. In the place of mounting a huge work force of 200 or more people to go out and cover the parish with calls for pledges, we are trusting our congregation this year by mailing out pledge cards with the full expectation that they will be returned in very substantial numbers, without the need of a personal call. Something in me makes me very nervous about that. That's the worrying part of me. The only calls we will make will be on those whose responses have not been received by November 21st. We hope that that will be a very few calls indeed. Our real hope is that you will mail your pledge card in or, better still, bring it with you to church next Sunday, Loyalty Sunday, and offer it to God as a part of our worship next week. We will save an enormous amount of time on the part of canvassers, time better spent on other things in this church, when we return our pledges on our own initiative. We trust you to do that out of your own commitment.

To help us with that, this morning I want to talk briefly about this church and the ministry of this church.

The point of departure I want to take is to look at our budget and see where our money, your gifts to God through this church, are used in ministry.

The budget of this church for this year is $643,000. That's a great deal of money, and with it comes a great deal of responsibility to use it effectively, a responsibility that the vestry and staff of this church take very seriously.

Of that income, 93 percent comes from the pledges you and I make annually. We have been blessed with a small endowment which faithful people, who love this church as you do, have given to us. That endowment and all other sources of income we have, put together, provides us with 7 percent of our annual income. That means that what we are able to do in ministry here we are able to do, to an overwhelming degree, because you and I, the current membership of Christ Church, provide for it through our annual pledge.

And what do we try to do? The priorities of the parish are clearly seen in our budget.

The highest single priority in our ministry here is in outreach. Thirty-one percent of our total income, the largest single portion of our budget, is in our outreach. This is the ministry that you and I undertake as Christians in our city, in our diocese, and beyond our diocese, into the world! Jesus said, "Go ye into all the world," and we try conscientiously to do that from this parish. The most helpful thing to me as I try to understand this is to see the faces of the people whose needs we try to serve outside the walls of this buildings.

There are the faces of seminary students, whose call to the priesthood has been validated by the Church and on whose training and leadership in the future the Church will depend. This fall we expect to have four candidates for the ministry from this parish, two in their senior year and two entering seminary for their beginning year.

I see the faces of drug addicts, the lines of decay beginning to fade because they have been snatched out of a living death by Victory Outreach and the Palmer Drug Abuse Program.

I see the faces of young people who have lost their way beginning to see a new way through Faith Ranch.

I see the faces of people whose marriages have been enriched and sometimes saved from destruction by superior counseling at the Ecumenical Center.

I see the faces of the children of this neighborhood, drawn here each summer to join our parish children in Vacation Bible School to learn, to play, and to be loved by the tender hand and warm smile of this church reaching out to them.

And I see the faces of Mexican children, whose language I do not even understand, smiling that expectant, friendly smile, in spite of living in sub-poverty conditions. And, in part through the efforts of our people to provide medical care, basic homemaking skills, and the love of Jesus Christ for them, I also see the possibility that some of their childlike expectations will be more adequately met as they grow up.

And I see so much more—people in small mission churches being served by clergy whose support comes largely from the diocese and, in part, because we support our diocese generously.

In all there are twenty-one separate outreach projects in which we here at Christ Church have a hand in extending the ministry of Jesus Christ. And I do not see them being disappointed by us in the year ahead. This ministry is our single largest priority, and we are all a part of it.

The second highest priority, taking 30 percent of our budget, is in the people we employ to carry out our ministry as professional staff people. These are the familiar faces of our clergy and the other professional people whose expertise and skill we use and enjoy in Christian Education, Lay Ministry, and Music.

Leadership with vision, energy, and commitment is the thing on which effective programs will always turn. I am very grateful to acknowledge the superior quality of the people who have been gathered to the staff of this church. Our skills are different. Our interests are different. Our experience varies. But our commitment to ministry, and our dedication to serve the Lord in this congregation is shared. It is a joy to me to work in and with the skills and dedication of these fine people. I have to confess to you that if I am anything I am realistic about the demands and the opportunities for ministry in this church. My realism leads me to say that the future for ministry in this place in and through our staff is as bright now as it has ever been.

I am also moved to digress just a moment to add something else. The ministry of leadership is profoundly enhanced by the support, the love, the acceptance, the work, the moral support, and the personal friendship extended by a congregation. In twenty-eight years of ministry I have never been in a congregation where that support has been as freely and abundantly given as it is given here by you. For myself, and I am sure I speak for your whole staff, I want you to know how much that means to us and how grateful we are for it. When we extend ministry you are also a part of that.

Our third priority, based on our budget, is in our buildings. Fourteen percent of our total income is used to maintain and keep this building in the physical shape that makes it usable, and a place we can be proud of in this community. If we neglect our buildings, John Greer never lets us get away with it for long. When we are tempted to be preoccupied with beautifying our building beyond our real need, the vestry will not let us get away with that. The mix that provides loving care without wasting our resources on luxury is the ideal we seek and the reality with which we live.

So what remains after we have spent 75 percent of our budget on outreach, on leadership people, and on this beautiful facility in which and out of which we can minister in the name of Christ?

What is left are all the enormous number of things we need to do that we are called to do together. Secretaries whose quick hands on typewriters and the mimeograph and whose pleasant voices on the telephone keep the wheels of completed work greased. Machines and reams of paper and shelves stocked with Sunday School curriculum and sheets and sheets of music and meals that are served and countless pounds of coffee that enhance the quality of our fellowship. Without any of that, the whole works would grind to a painful stop.

But when it moves, as it does—when it works in a myriad of ways to minister to the needs of people, because of your increased pledge and mine—you are part of that ministry! You are there when and where your church is there reaching out in the name of Christ. Indeed, if you were not there, your church would not be there either!

Recently some people from another part of the country sat in our congregation. I didn't know them and they had never been here before. About two weeks afterward one of them wrote me a letter about that one Sunday here. In part this is what was said:

"I have seldom been in a church as warm and loving as I saw that Sunday. Perhaps I can say it best using the word 'joyful.' I sensed that wonderful spirit of joy in being together on a beautiful Sunday morning in order to worship. Thank you for an uplifting and encouraging experience that I will long remember. God bless you in the ministry of your whole congregation."

Reading that I was tempted to be proud. But soon my pride turned to gratitude. Indeed, God has blessed us together in Christ Church. And I know, as we all are not proud but grateful, and as we all respond generously in our pledges, he will continue to bless us in the year ahead. Amen.

Exhibit 13

"The Greatness of a Church"
Stewardship: Presenting both the Challenge
and the Ministry of the Parish

This morning we enter the second week of our three-week stewardship program here at Christ Church. Last week in our sermon time I tried to say something about our outreach ministry, something about the demand that is laid upon every Christian church to go unto all the world and preach the Gospel. Now this morning we want to turn to look at our parish church to see the nature and reason for our ministry together. Next Sunday, November 7th, at all of our services every family in this parish will be given an opportunity to make a financial commitment to God through this parish on a pledge card. Following those services next week, fifteen teams of workers will go out to call on those who have not pledged in church. Then following the completion of our pledging, our vestry will take up the task of creating a budget for ministry in this place for next year.

So this morning in the middle of all that, we turn to look at Christ Church and at our life together here. We begin in what might seem to be a peculiar place.

Some months ago an article appeared in a very fine monthly magazine. It was their bicentennial issue and it was about life as we know it in the United States today. One article was titled "Great American Churches." There were six churches featured, most of them in the Eastern part of the country. The burden of the descriptions of these churches had to do with their long histories and the place they held in the history of our country. It was a very interesting article, but somehow it left me both dissatisfied and thoughtful—dissatisfied because I wasn't really convinced that a great and long history alone made for a great church, and thoughtful because it made me begin to wonder what does make a church great. I even particularized that to wonder what makes Christ Church a great church.

This morning I would like to suggest just two things to you that make up at least the beginning of an answer to those questions.

The first thing I'd like to suggest is this. The greatness of any church is not in the membership of the Church but in the Lord of the Church.

Jesus had pursued his ministry for as much as two years. One day, alone with his disciples, Jesus put this question to them. "Who do men say that I am?" And they answered him, "People are saying you are a prophet. You are John the Baptist risen from the grave. You are Elijah returned." And then, Jesus asked them, "But who do you say that I am?" After a moment's silence Peter answered for them all. "You are the Christ, the Son of the living God." And then Jesus said this: "I tell you, you are Peter, and on this rock·I will build my church. And the powers of hell shall not prevail against it."

Now, much has been made of these words over the generations. But there is no question of what they mean. The Church is built on a rock, and that rock is our faith that Jesus is the Christ and the Son of the living God. A great parish church derives its greatness from the faith of its people in Jesus Christ, the Son of God.

Someone, some time ago wrote what is now a very famous description of Jesus, titled "One Solitary Life."

> Here is a man who was born in an obscure village, the child of a peasant woman. He grew up in another obscure village. He worked in a carpenter's shop until he was thirty. And then for three years he was an itinerant preacher. He never wrote a book. He never held an office. He never owned a home. He never had a family. He never went to college. He never traveled more than 200 miles from the place where he was born. He had no credentials except himself. While still a young man the tide of popular opinion turned against him. He was turned over to his enemies. He was tried. He was executed as a common criminal between

two thieves. His executioners gambled for the only piece of property he ever owned. He was buried in a borrowed grave. Nineteen wide centuries have come and gone. But I am far within the mark when I say that all the armies that ever marched, and all the navies that were ever built, and all the parliaments that ever sat, and all the kings that ever reigned, put together, have not affected the life of man upon this earth as much as that one solitary life.

Indeed, no solitary life has affected your life and mine as much as the life of this person we call Jesus, the Son of the living God.

The other afternoon, after a particularly busy day, I stood out in front of this church building gazing up at that beautiful figure of Christ that is now above our entrance. It was raining, and the leaves of the trees above had fallen, to make a mess of the sidewalk and the empty stairs. The contrast between the figure of Christ above and the dirty sidewalks below suddenly grabbed me. This is the Church. This is our church. Sometimes, like that sidewalk, a little messy. Sometimes not as friendly as we ought to be. Sometimes not as smart, not as faithful, not as courageous as we ought to be. Sometimes pedestrian and dull in what we do. And sometimes absolutely magnificent and powerful.

But, then, I thought, this is not our church. It is his church. And when we are less than we could be he makes up for our lack. When we are what we might be he blesses the deed and multiplies it.

Well, the rain chased me away from the sidewalk. But that's when I knew that this morning I must say to you that the first mark of a great parish church is the heartfelt faith of its people that believes and accepts in its life Jesus Christ as the Son of the living God. This is the rock upon which we are founded, the person within our corporate life against whom the gates of hell shall never prevail. The greatness of a church is not in the membership of the Church but in the Lord of the Church.

That first mark is followed by a second. The second mark of

a great parish is that, in that faith, it be a parish dedicated to serve.

Once again, Jesus was with his disciples, now in the Upper Room at the Last Supper. Following the meal a discussion came up among the disciples as to who was to be regarded as the greatest among them. Hearing the discussion, Jesus said to them, "The Kings of the Gentiles exercise lordship over them. . . . But let it not be so among you. Rather let the greatest among you be as the youngest, and the leader as one who serves. For who is greater, one who sits at table or one who serves? But I am among you as one who serves."

Not authority, not power, not being served, but greatness falls upon the person who serves others. And following that example, any parish church that would be great must be a parish that serves.

Christ Church has tried to follow that example. In 1976, out of all of the resources we have available to us through our budget, we have committed ourselves as a parish to give almost 35 percent of our income to serve the needs of human life in our diocese and in our city. In the past two years the diocese raised almost half a million dollars in support of special projects outside their budget. Of that amount, almost 20 percent was given by people in and through Christ Church.

We have tried to follow that example. But it is not financial statistics but people who tell that story best. We recently received this letter from a family in our city.

> I am writing to thank you for all the good work you do with children. My son, Pedro, was fortunate to have attended Project OLE and Camp Bishop Elliott on a scholarship from your church. My daughter was a teacher's aide at Project OLE. Pedro and Elizabeth haven't stopped talking about all the wonderful things they did. They sing the songs they learned there. Pedro says he will never, never forget about this summer. Elizabeth hated being paid because she received so much more than she gave. So that is why I write and thank you for making my children so happy by sharing so much with them, and to let you know that

all your good work hasn't been in vain. Thank you so much, and thank God for people who care.

A great church is a church that cares enough to serve.

Yet there is more. A young boy was picked up in this city by the police at age eleven for stealing hubcaps from a car. At age twelve he was truant from school. At age fourteen he was picked up again for purse-snatching. At age seventeen he was finally picked up for drug possession. At that time he was well on his way to being addicted to heroin. Two years ago he was placed in the care of a group of committed Christians to work at getting off his drug habit. Equally important, he began to work on himself, to change his attitudes and feelings about himself so drugs would no longer be necessary for him to stay alive. Today I understand that that young man is clean and now works the streets trying to help others like himself. The Christian group to whom he was committed is called Victory Outreach, a ministry in the west side of this city supported in part by this church.

A great church is a church that cares enough to serve.

Still there is more. A year ago a woman in this city was divorced. It was a traumatic experience, one she never sought nor wanted. But it happened. For one year she struggled to understand this rejection, this devastating blow to her ego and to her family life. For a time she blamed and hated herself for what had happened. For a time she blamed the world for putting her here. For a time she even considered ending it all. This fall, through a friend, she came reluctantly to a meeting of divorced people held in this church. She describes that meeting as the first lifeline she found in a whole year. She still attends that group every week without missing, and she still has a long way to go. But she isn't afraid any more. She's even learning to like herself again and is looking forward to each new day again. A miracle? Perhaps. But a ministry supported by and through this church.

A great church is a church that cares enough to serve.

These are a bare beginning of the many things done in and through this church. Surely everything we try to do here is not as dramatic, and certainly not as successful, as these. And if we added up all the things that we do, that would be a bare beginning of what needs to be done and must be done and can be done in ministry in and through this church in the name of Jesus Christ.

When we do any of it, you are there, too, doing it through your stewardship gift to God through this church.

A Japanese Christian once wrote these words that have always seemed appropriate to me when I think about the corporate ministry of the Church that we have together to share. He wrote this:

> I cannot invent new things,
> Like airships which sail on silver wings;
> But today a wonderful thought
> In the dawn was given, and the
> Stripes on my robe shining from wear
> Were suddenly fair, bright with light
> Falling from heaven, gold and silver
> And bronze from the windows of Heaven.
> And the thought was this:
> That a secret plan is hid in my hands;
> That my hand is big—big because of this plan.
> That God, who dwells in my hand,
> Knows this secret plan—of the things
> He will do for the world—using my hand.

When this church ministers in God's name, it is your hand that God uses, for through your stewardship gift, you are there too.

A great church is a church that cares enough to serve.

Perhaps the conclusion of what we are trying to say is in this incident. Many years ago an evangelist was holding a great night meeting in Soldiers Field in Chicago. He was preaching on personal commitment to Jesus Christ. And in the middle of his sermon he stopped and asked that all the great high tower lights that flooded this huge stadium be turned out. They were, plunging this throng of people into darkness. Then he said, "Everyone of you take out a match and light it." And slowly but surely little flickering lights began to shine, first here and then there, until, in a moment that stadium was bathed in light. His point was dramatically made on the difference that just one light, gathered with many other single lights, could make.

Perhaps that is our point as well. This parish is one light in a dark world of need. We cannot do it all, but we can and will do something. I don't know if this is a great parish. I guess I don't spend too much time thinking about that. I do know that a great parish does have at least these two marks.

It is a parish where its people hold fast the faith of Jesus Christ as the Son of God. In that faith, it is a parish that cares enough to serve.

I do pray that we are growing and will continue to grow in that kind of greatness in the name of the Lord. Amen.

Exhibit 14

"Why, After All, Should I Give?"
Stewardship: Motives for Giving

This morning we stand before the very practical, earthy, and concrete event called stewardship time. Over the years, clergy and churches have called this by all kinds of names. We have called it the *Every Member Canvass, Loyalty Sunday, Commitment Time,* and *Stewardship Week.* I suspect that there are members of every parish, including this one, who, wanting to limit their religious commitments to words only and no action, have thought of other less complimentary names for this event as well.

As I have thought about the significance of our stewardship this year, another name for it has come to me. I would like to call it *Enablement Week.* This is the time when, by our financial commitments to God through this church, we enable the ministry of this church, we arm that ministry to be effective for Jesus Christ in this world. Through the process of enabling our church we also enable ourselves to be effective ministers in Christ's name through this church.

This enabling process begins this morning and climaxes next Sunday when, in all of our services of worship, we will be given the opportunity to make our commitment to God on a pledge card. For those who do not pledge in church, an army of 130 canvassers will make calls in our homes in the following ten days. Our hope and prayer is that by Thanksgiving Day we will be able to give great thanks to God for your response and begin building a budget for ministry in this place in the year ahead.

As some of you know, I have been a Stewardship Consultant for our national church for the past six years. In that role, I have conducted stewardship seminars for clergy and vestries literally in every corner of the nation. In these seminars I have asked these people to wrestle with one very basic question, and it's the question I would like to pose to you this morning. Why should anyone give anything at all to God through the Church? What claim does God have, or does the Church have, on any of us that allows for a serious asking of our financial sharing through the Church? Why should you give anything at all to God through the Church?

Having posed the question, I would like to suggest two answers for all of us to chew on this week as we think of our stewardship.

The first is simple, direct, and concrete. We are asked to give to God through this church because this church needs our giving if its ministry in the name of God is going to be effective.

Recently, someone telephoned me to ask if Christ Church could respond to a sudden and clearly legitimate need. This person asked for a sizable amount of money. I said that we were able and willing to do part of what was needed but could not do it all. The silence on the other end of the line was then followed by the comment, "Oh, I thought Christ Church was a rich parish."

I had heard the comment before, more than once. After I hung up the phone, I began to ponder it a little. Indeed, we are a rich parish—rich in the Spirit, rich in the commitment of our people to Christ, rich in the enthusiasm with which we go about our ministry. And I thought, yes, we are rich in dollars, too, given by dedicated people.

But we are rich in another way, too, in a way that tends to keep us poor. Our commitments to be a live, vital parish evangelically, educationally, pastorally, and in outreach are deep and extensive. Because of these commitments we spend our dollars carefully and effectively. But every year we spend them all, right down to the last few dollars, to arm our ministry with strength and make our work in Jesus' Name sing a "Gloria" to God.

That means that every year as we consider our ministry together, the need for committed and increased giving continues to be strong.

Did you know, for example, that 90 percent of our income annually comes from your pledges and mine? Something just over 9 percent comes from invested endowment funds. Sometimes when I think about our overwhelming dependence on annual pledges, I get a little frightened. But then I know that it is right to be dependent and to trust in God and in you for our ministry. I want to be just a little specific this morning. As we look ahead there are some needs we can see already. Christ Church is, and has been for some years, the largest single support for the ministry of our diocese and its bishop. Next year the diocese is again looking to us for that kind of leadership support. Our buildings, surely the most beautiful church buildings I have ever known in my twenty-five years of ministry—lovely, inspiring places to come to, to worship, to study, in which to work together and to serve the needs of others—need constant and increasing maintenance to keep them that way. Our staff, the finest group of Christian people I have had the privilege of sharing my ministry with, also need their work and skills recognized.

It sounds so mundane and common when I say it. But what are these things—the diocese as part of our outreach, our buildings, our people? They are mission churches and college ministry and new congregations and a bishop in whom and through whom the Spirit of Christ moves and speaks in this world. Our buildings, what is all this but a place, a focal point where we can come to learn and to speak and to listen and to make our commitments to him who is the Way, the Truth, and the Life. And our people, what are they? I would like to suggest that they are not just people who are skilled and dedicated whom we have come to know as good friends. They are a group of children in a Sunday School class learning about a God who loves them and cares about them. They are a class of adults wrestling with their faith and suddenly saying, "Oh, that's what it means to say, 'I believe. . . .'" They are another group in Bible study for whom the light begins to dawn in a whole new way about the meaning of Jesus Christ in their own life. They are a couple coming to be married, testing out their feelings about marriage with each other in an atmosphere that is created to be safe. They are people in the hospital facing pain and illness, who are visited and prayed with. They are thousands of things, thought about, prayed about, worried over and executed, so the Name of Jesus Christ can be more fully known and experienced among us. And they are people who know that as they do these things they are not alone because you are here with them, holding them up.

So why should anyone of us give anything at all to God through this church? Because we can enable these things to happen and because to make them happen effectively here this church needs our increased gifts for its ministry.

Then, there is another answer to that same question, equally as simple and direct and concrete. We are asked to give to God through this church because each of us needs to give to be spiritually whole.

One of the saddest stories in the New Testament is the one recorded in the seventeenth chapter of St. Luke. Jesus is going toward Jerusalem. As he went he was met by ten men, all victims of the dread disease leprosy. "Master, have mercy on us," they cried. And when he saw them Jesus had compassion on them and, in a single stroke, he healed them all. Human wreckage was turned into health. It was a miracle.

But then we read, "And one of them, when he saw that he was healed, turned and with a loud voice glorified God, and fell down on his face at his feet, giving him thanks." And here is the sad part. "And Jesus answering said, 'Were there not ten cleansed? But where are the other nine?' "

Jesus' words are laden with all the disappointment and the frustration and the weariness that he must often have felt when people failed to respond to his gifts by giving thanks.

Surely here is a clue to the deepest answer to the question we posed at the beginning. You and I are asked to give because it is one of the ways that we can give thanks to our great and merciful God.

Sometimes I have thought a little bit about what God has given to me. When I do, I usually think about now, the present moment, and about what God is doing in my life now. And there is always something there. But occasionally I get more basic and think of other things.

The gift of life and the air I breathe to sustain life in me. That is from God. This good earth in which to live my life, its vast resources tht can be tapped to make life prosperous and good. That is from God. And not for me only but for you as well.

Very recently I have learned another way to see the gifts of God that I have received.

In a group we recently did an exercise together. We were asked to think about a person who had been very influential in our lives. And then, with that person in mind, we were asked to identify what this person had done, how this person had behaved with us to make us remember him or her so fondly. We put all these behaviors up on a large piece of paper and considered them together. Then we were asked the question: To which of these things in our experience could we legitimately attach the Name of Jesus? Which of these things did we believe Jesus Christ did with us and for us? For me it was an over-whelming feeling to be able to put the Name of Jesus in front of every one of them. Jesus listens to me. Jesus cares about me. Jesus challenges me. Jesus values my life as a life of worth. Jesus encourages me to be the best I can be.

While this was not our purpose then, I went home with a heart full of thanksgiving to God for what he is and does for me. Henry Ward Beecher wrote it this way.

> If one should give me a dish of sand and tell me that there were particles of iron in it, I might look for them with my eyes, and search for them with my clumsy fingers, and be unable to detect them; but let me take a magnet and sweep through it, and how it would draw to itself the most invisible particles by the mere power of attraction.

The unthankful heart, like my fingers in the sand, discovers no mercies; but let the thankful heart sweep through the day, and as the magnet finds the iron, so it will find, in every hour, some heavenly blessings; only the iron in God's sand is gold.

How can I express my thanks? There are a thousand ways. But, I am absolutely certain that one way I must give thanks is to give what I can back to him in return. It is a must for me to be spiritually whole.

So, we return whence we came. Why should anyone give anything at all to God through the Church? This week, as we all consider our stewardship response, I would submit two answers.

We give because the Church, to be effective, needs our increased giving.

We give because we need, for our spiritual wholeness, to give thanks to God for his gifts.

Exhibit 15

"Now Concerning the Contributions
for the Saints ..."
Stewardship: On Systematic Giving

For the past several weeks in our Church News, and last Sunday in our sermon, the focus of our attention has been on our stewardship. All this has pointed toward Loyalty Sunday, toward this morning when all of us are being invited to make our commitment to God through this church on a pledge card. In these weeks we have really tried to say three very simple things. The clergy families and some of our lay families have tried to say in print how we think about our own stewardship. And we have tried to do that, not because we are leaders of this parish, but simply as struggling Christians who have thought about our giving, prayed about it, and come to decide about it as responsible Christians before God. Last Sunday in our sermon I tried to say two other things. First, we are asked to give because this parish has some needs for ministry in this place, in our diocese and the world that we must meet in the year ahead. Secondly, and far more deeply, we tried to say that we are asked to give because to be spiritually whole and thankful to God for his many blessings we must give responsibly.

Now we come to the day when each of us must make a decision for ourselves on our pledge card. This week, as I have thought about myself and our family and what we will do on our pledge card, I felt the need to go back to the fundamentals, to search the Scripture and see what the Bible has to say about our stewardship. I was led to the fifteenth and sixteenth chapters of I Corinthians, that portion we read as our second lesson this morning. There are three things that came out of it for me that I would like to share with you and about which I ask your thought and prayer before you make your pledge.

The first is this. My stewardship and yours is not a matter of money so much as it is a matter of our spiritual life.

In I Corinthians chapter fifteen Paul is writing on the great Christian proclamation of life after death. It is a beautiful and deeply reassuring passage. "Lo, I tell you a mystery. We shall not all sleep, but we shall all be changed. For the trumpet shall sound, and the dead shall be raised incorruptible." And Paul then raises this great proclamation to poetic heights. "Death is swallowed up in victory. O death, where is thy victory? O death, where is thy sting? Thanks be to God who gives us the victory through our Lord Jesus Christ."

Then, without missing a beat or even pausing for a breath, Paul goes right on from this magnificent proclamation to say, "Now, concerning the contributions for the saints. . . ." And he gives these Corinthians very clear and detailed instructions about how to share their possessions.

Reading those two things together, which years ago I would have thought were strange bedfellows, it struck me once again that what we believe and how we respond to God's great gift of life after death, and what we do on our pledge card are not separate matters. They are really two parts of the same thing. Both have to do with our faith, with our belief in Jesus Christ as the Lord of our life, both here and hereafter.

Surely, that is one of the most important reasons that Jesus spent so much time talking about the relationship of people and their money. Jesus knew that the real key to a person's faith, the key to what a person really believes, is in the way he or she thinks about his or her possessions.

In the twelfth chapter of Mark Jesus is standing by the door of the Temple and he saw how many came in and gave their offerings. Some gave much because they had much. But a widow came in and gave two mites, a very small offering, but it was all that she had. Jesus called his disciples to him and commended the widow for her gift, not because it was going to do all that much for the Temple but because in relation to what she had it told him so much about what her values were, what kind of faith she possessed.

In contrast to that, there was very little that provoked Jesus to lower valleys of disappointment than when honest, upright, believing people professed their great devotion but did not follow that by sharing thankfully out of what they possessed. Jesus spoke with obvious disappointment about Dives, the rich man who daily walked past Lazarus begging at his gate and did not help. He spoke with judgment about the rich farmer who with a bumper crop could think of nothing to do with it but to build bigger barns in which to store it. Or most deeply for me, Jesus comments with scorn in his voice about the most vocal and obvious religious people of his day, the Pharisees, of whom he said, "The scribes and and Pharisees sit on Moses' seat, so practice and observe whatever they tell you, but not what they do, for they preach but do not practice. . . ." No preacher ever stands in a pulpit without those words stabbing at that preacher's conscience. By the same token, no Christian can stand before his or her faith without those words probing in his or her heart.

The story is told of a rural congregation in which one of the member families had been burned out in a terrible fire. The pastor called the congregation to prayer at the site of the fire. They all appeared save one family who came very late. That family arrived in their wagon, the back of which was laden with food, clothing, and furniture. The pastor chided them about being late and missing the prayer meeting. But the father of the family responded, "Pastor, we brought our prayers in the wagon."

Our faith is a matter of our belief, a matter of saying our prayers. And it is also a matter of our contributions for the saints. My stewardship and yours is not so much a matter of money as it is a matter of our spiritual life.

Then St. Paul leads us to another thing. When we consider our stewardship we have a need to return to God out of the blessings we have received in a systematic way. In this same passage, Paul, having reminded these Corinthians of their spiritual need to make contributions to the saints, goes on to say this. "Now concerning the contribution for the saints: as I directed the churches of Galatia, so you also are to do. *On the first day of every week*, each of you is to put something aside and store it up, as he may prosper, so that contributions need not be made when I come."

Paul was on one of his missionary journeys, writing ahead as it were, to the churches he planned to visit. One of the concerns he carried on his heart as he traveled was the persecution and the economic deprivation being suffered by the new Christians in Jerusalem. Jerusalem was the heart of Judaism, the place where it was most difficult to be a Christian. And so, Paul, burdened by their trials, was asking other Christians to give to help them in their need. That expression of concern for them cannot be effective, Paul said, if it were to only a sudden burst of generosity when he arrived. To be effective, it must be systematic. *"On the first day of every week*, each of you is to put something aside. . . ."* Giving is not a hit-or-miss affair. To be effective it must be disciplined and systematic.

The need for some kind of systematic discipline is so clear in so many things that we do. The illustrations are abundant.

For example, I am put to shame personally by the regular disciplines that some of you undertake for your health. There are men and women in this congregation who jog every single day to keep fit. I am equally impressed with some of the women in this church, of whom my wife has now become one, who work out in some fashion two or three times a week to keep the body fit. In all of that, of course, the basic principle is not that you do it but that you do it systematically and with regularity. In any other fashion it would not work. A hit-or-miss system in physical fitness is not effective for your health.

Or, on another level entirely, in a family and a marriage one of the things that I have learned is that it is not enough simply to be there and to say to those around us in our homes, "I love you." Somehow, and in some systematic, pre-planned way, time must be kept and actively planned that will illustrate, that will concretely demonstrate that when we say those words, "I love you," we really mean what we say. For as many years as I can remember I have committed Friday night to be my night

with my wife. We often enjoy spending that night in the com-
pany of other people. But as far as we are able, that night is our
night to be social. The business of the church which occupies
so much of our time and energy seldom is allowed to interfere.
It is one of the ways we try to pay attention to each other and
to avoid taking each other for granted. I have learned that I
must be systematic about that if I am going to be able to
maintain an effective relationship with my family.

All that is said to suggest what St. Paul suggests, that our
giving also needs to be a systematic discipline. For us there is
great significance in our coming to church to worship each
week. We come here every week to say our prayers, to offer our
sins and failures to God, and to receive his forgiveness in the
body of this church. There is something special to us in coming
up out of our seats to this altar rail to be fed in the Eucharist,
and even in going down to the parish hall and just talking with
people in the informality of the coffee hour. In the context of
those things, done regularly, it also has great meaning to us,
with the same regularity, to make the offering of our substance
to God through this church. As far as the church is concerned,
it does not really matter how our offerings are made, but for our
gift to carry the maximum effectiveness for us, to let it be a
weekly reminder of our blessings from God, a weekly reaffirma-
tion of our commitment to God, a weekly reminder of the joy
and satisfaction we feel about giving, we must do it systematically and regularly. We find St. Paul's admonition helpful in our
spiritual life. "*On the first day of each week,* each of you is to
put something aside and store it up," to be given.

Then, finally, there is a third thing St. Paul says. Our giving
needs to be based, not ultimately on any need we respond to but
on what we have been given, that is, based on our income. "On
the first day of every week, each of you is to put something aside
and store it up, *as he has prospered.*" That leads us right to the
heart of the matter for Christians. We give because we have first
been given to.

The gifts of God are so perfectly obvious, given a moment's

thought. Life, breath, a talent, a skill to use, a good earth in which to use what we have, these have all been given. Beyond that, consider the less tangible things, things like prayer and sacraments and the fellowship of a church, as vehicles of reaching out to the God who is also reaching out to us. Ultimately, consider the salvation we have in Jesus Christ. These too we haven't earned, but they are given.

Thus, when we are asked to give, we give in return from what we have received. St. Paul's phrase is to give *"as we have prospered."* The best Christian translation of all that is called *proportionate giving.* It goes like this. To be responsible with ourselves and God, to give out of thanksgiving as we have prospered, we take our income, which is the most concrete measure of what we have, and apply to that income whatever portion we feel is the conscientious, responsible percentage we wish to return to God through this church.

Many Christians, including many in this parish, have been tithers, that is, they return 10 percent of their income to God. Others have become modern tithers, giving 5, 6, 7 percent to God through the Church and another percentage to God through many charities outside the Church. Many, many others here have begun at 3 or 4 percent and have raised that portion by ½ percent or 1 percent in each year as they grow in their stewardship. But whatever you feel in your heart is your responsible portion, the important thing is that we see our pledge as reflecting our income and our sense of responsibility—a gift, in Paul's words, *"as you have prospered."* That is proportionate giving and that is the heart of Christian stewardship.

Well, my Bible search this week led me to St. Paul, and Paul has led all of us to consider:

That our pledge is not so much a matter of money as it is a matter of our spiritual life.

That returning to God in our giving is most effective when it is systematic, "on the first day of each week."

That Christian giving begins as we base it on income "as we have prospered."

How you respond to all that is now a matter between you, your family, and your God.

Let us pray.

> Prosper, O Lord, the work of our hands in this place as we enlist ourselves and our substance in loving ministry in the name of Christ. Help us to see that we are unworthy of your blessings unless we share them with others. Open your eyes to see the high calling of Christian stewardship and inspire us to count it a joy to arm our ministry and bring the Gospel to every corner of your world. And this we pray through Jesus Christ our Lord. Amen.

Exhibit 16

"Possessions and Sacrificial Giving"
Stewardship: On Giving

For the past several weeks we have been preparing for our annual stewardship program here at Christ Church. A committee has been hard at work. The vestry and the staff have already been canvassed as leaders in this parish. Captains have been chosen and trained, canvassers chosen and trained. Now on these two Sundays, today and next Sunday, it is my privilege to talk with all of you.

During the year we talk a great deal about the stewardship of our time and talent, both desperately needed in this church and in our city, given on behalf of this church by its members. In the fall our emphasis and concern falls to the stewardship of our material resources, our money, also desperately needed to carry out the ministry of this church.

At this time of year, every year, I am always tempted to fall back on the old ways and talk about the needs of the church. I could make a strong case for giving on that basis. For example, I could tell you that 94 percent of all this church's income comes from the pledges of our families. Less than 6 percent of our annual income comes from endowments and other gifts. What you and I give is what this church lives on.

But I do not want to pursue that because that's to become a fund raiser and our real need is talk about stewardship.

Recently I was in another parish to speak on this subject. In the discussion that followed, this question was raised. "Why don't we just put out a budget and then go out and raise the money to support it?" What I told them was this. "If all I wanted to do was raise money that's exactly what I would do—build a budget and then go out and sell it. But stewardship is so much more than raising money. It's an attitude about the reality of our life and the reality of our relationship with God."

As I pursued that with them, I'd also like to pursue that theme with you this morning. To do so I want to say two fundamental things about Christian stewardship.

The first begins with a question. In modern American life, what is the single most prominent thing that you and I will spend more time thinking about, worrying about, planning for, and working for than any other single thing?

The answer for the vast majority of us is money. How to earn it, how to save it, how to accumulate it. How to make it stretch to meet our needs, where to invest it, how to protect it, and where and to whom we will spend it and give it. You and I will spend more of our waking hours in these pursuits than any other single thing that we do.

The reason we have become so preoccupied with that in modern America is that, wrapped up in our ability to generate income, to have money and what money will buy, is a tremendous amount of our sense of personal success or lack of it, our sense of self-worth or lack of it, our sense of well-being or lack of it, our sense of power or lack of it. In our society, who are the people who are judged the most successful? Clearly, it is those people who have succeeded financially.

Because money and success are so tied together in our society, and because you and I so desperately want to have that sense of well-being and success that money brings, people will steal for money, cheat for money, lie for money, use money or withhold money as a way to punish other people, and if we have it, will be tempted to flaunt it in ways obvious and subtle.

Why else is it that when we or our children go out to buy jeans nowadays, we buy them with some designer's name on the hip pocket? Or why do we buy running shoes with some maker's name or symbol in the back? Or why do we wear neckties with a designer's initials at the bottom, or blouses or dresses with the proper designer's name on the front or, at least, in the neck label? Or why do we buy knit shirts and tennis shorts with some animal figure on them. Alligators are in, I'm told. Foxes don't make it in the better circles.

We buy things like that, and pay premium prices for them, because we want ourselves and the world to know that we have the money to afford them and the good sense to wear what is in style. We can carry this into a thousand other illustrations—the cars we drive, the houses we live in, the clubs we belong to, or wish we could. You can take it almost as far as you want.

Now my point is not to say that this is true for everyone, although for a lot of us, and I do not exempt myself, it is true. My point is to say that this is the kind of power that money has. The extent to which you and I get taken into measuring our sense of success and well-being, our sense of personal power and self-worth, in financial terms, is the extent to which you and I live in a prison made of money and what money will buy.

With all of the integrity that I can muster, I would submit to you that there is another way. It is a way I discovered for myself some years ago and have continued to work at ever since.

When any one of us comes to really believe that what we have, we have directly or indirectly from the hands of a gracious, generous God; when we can begin to see that what we have, we have as a gift; when we can begin to see *ourselves* as the receivers of God's abundant generosity; and then, when we are able to respond to that generosity by returning to God a portion of what he has given us, set aside a responsible percentage of what we have, to give back to God through the Church—then it is possible for us to begin to see ourselves in a relationship with God in which we are trying to be a responsible partner. In that consciously sought-after relationship, our need for a sense of success about ourselves, a sense of self-worth, a sense of well-being is abundantly met and satisfied. Indeed, in the final analysis it is in that relationship alone that these precious and needed things will ever be found.

If I were to have to tell you about the development of my relationship with God, it would be here, in my struggle to make my stewardship choices, that it has grown and deepened more concretely than in any other way. When we sign our pledge card and sense our partnership with God—he as the giver and we as responsible givers in return—there is a sense that comes to us of power and well-being, of self-worth and success as human beings.

That has nothing to do with this church's need for money. It has a lot to do with our relationship with God, yours and mine. That's what stewardship is about.

Let me suggest one other basic thing this morning.

We hear a good deal about something called sacrificial giving. Usually we take that to mean that we need to dig a little deeper, give a little more than we intended, sacrifice a little so the Church will have enough.

I'd like to suggest that that is to misunderstand sacrifice. Let me try to suggest a better understanding of it this way.

In the Old Testament the Jewish people used sacrifices as a way to worship God. While they were in the wilderness during the Exodus, the people gathered at a place called "the tent of meeting" to offer sacrifice for the forgiveness of their sins. They were civilized enough not to use a human sacrifice. It was an animal sacrifice, in which the people took the most perfect lamb from their flock and offered it to God. That perfect lamb became a representative of all the people. In the sacrifice of one lamb, the very best lamb, the sins of *all the people* were taken away. In the gift of one, all the rest were hallowed, made holy and forgiven. A sacrifice was the giving of the best portion to God, so that the remainder could be made pure.

We see that sacrificial principle in operation in many other areas of our life.

God says to us, "I want to hallow and be part of all of your time no matter where you are or what you are doing. So what I want from you is a sacrifice, a portion of your time, given exclusively to me. Make me a sacrifice of your time so I can hallow and make all of your time blessed and useful." So God gave us a commandment, "Remember the sabbath day to keep it holy." By our dedicating one day in the week to him, he can bless all of the days of the week for us.

Or, to pull it down even closer to us. If you have a daily prayer discipline, you will understand what I am saying. When you give God a part of each day, in a prayer time, the whole remainder of the day is different somehow. God takes your sacrifice, your best portion that you give, and uses it to make the remainder qualitatively different. Frankly, the times when I am aware of that most are in those days when I fail to give God his time. Then, the day is different but not better.

That's a sacrifice, to give God the best portion so that the remainder can be hallowed and blessed.

The conversion of that to sacrificial giving is simple.

We are called to give God a sacrifice of our money, give to God the best portion, that is, give it first before other things. God, in his turn, will hallow and bless the remainder to make it adequate to meet all of our needs. That's the same thing that Jesus talked about when he said, "Give, and it shall be given unto you; good measure, pressed down, shaken together, running over will be put into your lap." That's sacrificial giving—giving our best portion, knowing that God will make the remainder adequate, and more than adequate, to meet our needs. The trick, of course, is for us to make the first move, to make our sacrifice so God can use it. But Christian stewardship is not a matter of money as much as it is a matter of taking that kind of risk in faith.

Next Sunday is Pledge Day, when we will be asked to make our commitment to God on a pledge card. I trust it will not be made because the church needs our money. Indeed the church does, and in as generous a way as we possibly can give it. But we give best when we give for a different reason. We give to be good stewards of God's gifts to us and so we can know the rewards of that vital partnership with him.

Exhibit 17

"A Man, Going on a Journey, Gave Talents . . ."
Stewardship: Time and Talent

One of the most familiar parables of Jesus is the one we call "the parable of the talents."

In spite of its familiarity I turn to it today because we have been praying and thinking about our fall stewardship program extensively in the past three months. This is not to be an Every Member Canvass sermon, but rather a stewardship sermon having to do with our stewardship of the time and talents. But that gets ahead of my story.

St. Matthew, chapter twenty-five, gives us the parable.

A man going on a journey left five talents with one servant, two talents with another, and one talent with the third. The servant with five talents traded them and made five more. The man with two earned two more. But the man with only one talent buried it in the ground for safekeeping. When the master returned he commended the servants who had used his gifts to increase them. But for the man who simply saved his one talent, the master had nothing but contempt and anger. "Cast the worthless servant into outer darkness; there men will weep and gnash their teeth."

Now, we have used that parable to suggest a great many things. While all people are equal in the sight of God, not all people have the same abilities or talents.

A maid was once called to account by her employer for her slovenly work. "Why, I can write my name in the dust here on this table," the woman protested. "Isn't that wonderful," the maid replied. "That's more than I can do. It just goes to show what an education can do for you."

We do not all have the same talents, either by quantity or in their quality.

We have said that judgment, therefore, is and will be based not on what we do in relation to what others do but in relation to what we ourselves could have done. One-talent people are not expected to produce five-talent results. Conversely, five-talent people may not be satisfied by being slightly more productive than two-talent people. "To whom much is given, much will be required."

These things we have said because they are true. I submit them almost by title this morning because you all know these things already. Now I'd like to try to take a broader view of the teaching of the parable and suggest three things about our stewardship of time and talent.

First, every talent we have and every moment of time we live is a gift of God.

You are quite accustomed to my standing here to say that our material wealth is a gift of God, and that when we come to our financial stewardship we need to return to God out of that which he has given us. But it is equally true that time and talent are gifts of God. The way we use our time and our talent needs to be seen as a very substantial way in which we can return to God of that which we have been given.

Recently my wife and I have searched for a painting to hang in our home. We haunted art galleries, a new experience for me, looking for something suitable. We did finally find something in our price range. But my major impression of the search was to stand in awe and near reverene of the tremendous talents of the artists whose work we saw. The color sense, the precision, the ability to see something and then to commit it to canvas almost overwhelmed me. I have no artistic ability at all unless you consider talking a lot as a talent. I am completely aware that perspiration is needed to bring the inspirational talent to a completed work. But the gift, the tremendous gift of artistic talent, is God's alone to give.

I could turn to music, or to the less obvious but equally clear gift of administrative business skill, or the analytical and imaginative skills of attorneys, or the visual skills of architects and builders, or the teaching talents of educators, or to the talent I see in people to be compassionate and caring with others. There are literally thousands of special talents among us that we have from God. In each, while we develop those talents by our own blood, sweat, and tears; the talent, what we call the innate ability, belongs to God, and we are blessed by having it loaned to us to use during our lifetime.

Time is no less a gift from God. Recently I sat with a man who had just recovered from a severe chest ailment. There was a point at which he could not breathe; his life hung in the balance. He was a young man, with plans and assumptions about the length of his days and what he would do with them, all of which for about two and a half minutes were in serious danger. The man recovered and is well. Once he got over the physical shock we talked about his reaction to it all. Among the things he said to me was this. "I understand for the first time that life and time are gifts. We think we have all the time in the world, and suddenly we know we don't." Then he laughed and said, "It sure made me aware of the proverb, 'Don't put off until tomorrow what you can do today.'"

That's the major teaching of the parable. What we have in time and talent we have been given and we are expected to use them as a return to God. "A man going on a journey, gave talents to his servants. . . ."

Then the parable goes on to say that with the time and talent we have been given we are expected to produce something of value for others.

The treatment of the one-talent man has always seemed a little harsh to me. "Cast the worthless servant into outer darkness." Surely, I have thought, a Lord who specializes in forgiveness and grace is a little out of character with such a harsh judgment. But the words remain and they do belong to Jesus. The judgment in the parable was not because the servant had tried and failed—that could have and would have been forgiven—but because he had never tried at all. The sin, if that's a good word, of the one-talent man was that he preferred to care for nothing but his own comfort, his own needs, his own well-being rather than risking any of that for others. His own need was to be so careful with his talent as to be safe, while Jesus' command was to produce.

Sometimes, as I go around trying to teach stewardship in other parishes, I invite them to consider this question. What would be missing—what of value would disappear from the community outside your church if the earth opened up at this moment and this church were to be swallowed up and be gone forever? It's a hard question and very threatening in a church that has lived primarily to itself. It's also a question that can be applied to an individual human life. What would be missing— what would disappear if we, you and I, were to be taken today from the face of the earth?

That's a terrible way to phrase the question. In terms of the parable it can be put this way. What are we producing for other people by and through our lives that no one else, by opportunity or ability, can produce? Because I preach to myself as well as to you, when I thought of the question I sat at my desk trying to frame an answer for my own life. The list was pitifully short, and the teaching of Jesus that we are here to produce something for others, hit home to me in a new way.

Last June Dr. Ernest Campbell, one-time Senior Pastor of Riverside Church in New York City, delivered a commencement address. He had just recently resigned that prestigious post at an unusually young age. He spoke of the mail he had received at the time of his early retirement, some of which was critical of his decision. In the context of Riverside Church's being one of the most prestigious pulpits in the world, he said, "A few have crassly put to me the question, 'Where will you go after you have been to Riverside?' The answer I give is always the same, 'Why, to any place where what I have and know and am can be a service to another.' "

Well, what about a question like that? What are we conscious of producing that is of value beyond ourselves, by and through the way we live this life that has been given to us? Jesus says in the parable that here is a critical question each of us must ask ourselves.

That all leads to a final lesson from the parable. As religious people, as church members, *where* are we to produce these things from the time and talent we have been given? The answer is twofold: in the world and in the church.

When I was young in the ministry I lived in a small southern Minnesota town. The time and talent of the people in that town were in great demand to meet a tremendous variety of community needs. But there was a church there, and a rather large one, where the pastor taught his people that whatever discretionary time they had was to be given to the church to the exclusion of the community. I had, and still have, great difficulty with that.

To be sure the church needs your time and talent, and we need a lot of it. We are not reluctant to ask for it—on committees, in the classrooms, in offices of various kinds, and as participants in all that we do here. In fact, the need of what you can give your church sometimes overwhelms me in its magnitude. I am seldom overwhelmed as much by anything else except by your generous willingness to give of your time and talent.

Someone wrote a paragraph that describes how important you are to your church.

> This story is about four people named Everybody, Somebody, Anybody, and Nobody. There was an important job to be done and Everybody was asked to do it. Everybody was sure that Somebody would do it. Anybody could have done it, but finally Nobody did it. Somebody was puzzled by that because it was Everybody's job. Everybody thought that Anybody could do it. Nobody realized that Everybody would not do it. It ended up that Everybody blamed Somebody, but Nobody blamed Anybody. And the job was left undone.

This church, as an institution, is not like the Marine Corps which advertises, "We need a few good men." We need a lot of people who are willing to invest their time and their talent in what needs doing here.

But, that said, the thrust of the parable is that it is in the world where we as Christians are primarily asked to produce—in our jobs, in our families, in our social life.

It seems to me that has far less to do with *what* we do than *how*, in what spirit, and with what quality we do what we do. It is significant that the parable is cast in the context of a business setting. The talents were money, one talent in the parable being worth about fifteen years of a laborer's wages. But I suggest to you that Jesus would not have been much moved by the sight of shrewd businesspersons, smart lawyers, brilliant physicists, competent office workers, or efficient housewives. I believe he is much moved to see godly businesspersons, godly lawyers, godly physicists, godly office workers and godly housewives—godly whatever. The challenge of the parable is the search for men and women whose supreme vocation is serving God and whose occupation is simply an adjective describing one place where that service is rendered.

Driving through Nebraska one time, I saw a church sign that advertised "Divine Service" and then listed the times of worship. The sign has always struck me as unfortunate. Divine worship happens on Sunday. Divine service happens on any day, in the office or the plant, among employers and employees, in civic committees and in our homes among our family, and in the lounge and grill at the country club. There is that which we are called to produce for others, so that the world, in ways however small or big, can be changed because we "Christians" have been there. Someone once said, "Be thoughtful in how you live. You may be the only Bible some people will ever read."

Marco Polo, who traveled from Venice to the Orient in the fourteenth century, told stories of the wonders he had seen there. Because these things were beyond the imagination of his people they accused him of lying. When he was dying at the age of seventy, his friends asked him to confess his lies since he was about to meet his Maker. The last words Marco Polo uttered were these: "I never told the half of it."

Nor can Christians tell half of what it feels like to honestly give themselves, their time and their talents, by conscious decision and in some conscientious measure, back into the service of God. It is freedom, joy, and confidence. It is part of our responsible stewardship. It is, in a word, to have a taste of that peace which passes understanding.

"A man going on a journey left talents with his servants. . . ."

And the Master commended the servants who had used his gifts to increase them.